FAITH and the POWER

of Healing

Rodgers Masuta

PROMINENT
BOOKS
EDGE

5830 E 2nd St, Ste 7000 #9983
Casper, WY 82609
USA

The life Secret... Will. Might. Belief. Receive it. Envision It. See The Finish Line. See The Victory. See The Glory. Give Thanks. Keep the Faith...

Remember. The mind is a powerful thing.

May 6, 2020

As I sit in my room at home here in Atlanta Georgia, still on contact isolation. It is 11pm, May 6, 2020. I am 4 days discharged from a renowned Atlanta area hospital, after a week on the 11th floor covid unit. I just received a whatsapp message from my sister (Choice) in Zimbabwe, the eldest of the six of us. All the message read was (Psalm 86:11–16). I must admit I come from a very religious and believing family. At times I disregard the verses and scriptures I receive from my family, there are so many to try to read them all. This time was different. I decided to check the verse out. Days prior I had made a deal, a bargain, a pledge with God, the morning of April 30 before the nurses or doctors came into my room for their rounds. (I will explain later). I went to my Bible app on my phone to look up the verses.

The Holy Bible, Authorized King James Version: "Teach me thy way, O LORD: I will walk in thy truth: Unite my heart to fear thy name. I will praise thee. O Lord my God, with all my heart: and I will glorify your name for evermore. For great is thy mercy toward me: and thou hast delivered my soul from the lowest hell. O God, the proud are risen against me, and the assemblies of violent men have sought after my soul: and have not set thee before them. But thou O Lord, art a God full of compassion, and gracious longsuffering, and plenteous in mercy and truth. O turn unto me, and have mercy upon me: give thy strength unto thy servant and save the son of thine handmaid. Verse 17 goes on to say. Shew me a token for good, that they which hate me may see it, and be ashamed: because thou, LORD has helped me, and comforted me.

I read these verses and told myself. This is exactly the conversation I had with God as I was gasping for air (oxygen) not knowing if I was going to make it or not, as I lay in that hospital bed, connected with several tubes, receiving continuous oxygen and Intravenous Therapy to help treat my condition. Pleading with God to save me and I will in turn tell the world of his healing powers and how powerful and amazing he is. "Lord save me, I will glorify your name." I spoke out loudly at least three times in my low energy voice as I squirmed in bed believing he would. **Jeremiah 17:14 ESV. Heal me, O LORD, and I shall be healed, save me, and I shall be saved, for you are my praise.**

DEDICATION

This book is inspired by many occasions that have happened in my life. I have seen the power of God in my life. The lowest and saddest moment of my life was when we lost the baby of our family on August 13, 2017. Tendai my baby, we had made many plans to live this life and enjoy each other, I have so many happy memories with you. I will cherish them all until we meet again. I miss you every single day. God needed and extra angel, I have questioned him why? Why you, but I have accepted. It was his will. I thank God for the 35 years he granted you to share with us on this earth. You were always smiling and bubbly, full of love and energy. So caring and compassionate. May your dear soul rest in peace. Tendai Chipo Precious Masuta. I miss you baby girl. Sleep in peace. I love you.

CONTENTS

PREFACE

A FEW DAYS ago I swear I thought it was over, I did not think I would wake up the next morning. I did not see myself live to see another day or next minute, but things suddenly turned around for me. Something in my head showed me a sign to say not yet. This is not your time to give up. I started seeing an army of prayer warriors, messages and encouragement from everywhere and unexpected sources, cousins, aunts, uncles, friends, my siblings and parents. This made me talk to God and believed there is no way he will disappoint his army and believers. The love and support and talking to mom and dad and their encouraging words and love made me say. I AM NOT GIVING UP! I could not do that to my mother or have my father bury another child. I rebuked the devil and premature death. I had to believe I was not going out this way. **Psalm 41:3 ESV. The Lord sustains him on his sickbed, In his illness you restore him to full health.** The night I got admitted and rushed to the Hospital via 911, that next 72 hours was my turning point. I had to keep fighting. On high oxygen artificial breathing, headaches, fevers, pain, gasping for air and to breathe at times. Having a conversation with the doctor the night before I removed the oxygen, about being escalated to the ICU unit, get intubated and be put on a ventilator if my blood oxygen level did not improve and I continued to need more oxygen. I was on the edge of either ICU or if lungs cleared and breathing and my dependency on oxygen improved, I would be on the right track and won't need the ventilator route. The prayers and God's grace gave me a second chance and more life, I felt the energy of the prayers and knew God will not disappoint his children. I had sudden wings, faith and belief. In my case I don't know, I cannot say I was given a second chance. I guess I should say, at least the 5th chance of this life. I have had several life and death situations and just by the brink of death. God has always been there to hold my hand and save me, and breathe life into me again.

I would be in isolation in my hospital room with no access to any physical outside world, except the nurses, doctors and technicians who were super geared and protected not to have any contact and maintain the isolation. The few times I had to be transferred to the x-ray and CT Scan, and ekg departments there on the Covid-19 unit, I kept seeing and hearing commotion, some patients getting CPR and being coded, overhead pages of emergencies in room xxxx. Clearly some people did not make it. I saw lifeless bodies and body bags being taken off the floor. This would be a sight the few times I had to be taken out of my isolation room to go to Ct scan and xrays departments. I would just say a prayer for their souls. On the tombstone of my little sister is the verse,

Isaiah 57:1–2 The righteous perish and no one takes it to heart, the devout are taken away, and no one understands that the righteous

are taken away to be spared from evil. Those who walk uprightly enter into peace, they find rest as they lie in death. These last 8 words of verse 2 have given me comfort with my sister, as I believe and love the fact that she will never feel pain or suffering on this earth again, as she sleeps in the Lord.

That is the same comfort and peace I believe all those who did not make it will not suffer again, they will never have pain or gasp and yearn for oxygen and struggle to breathe again. They are resting as they lie in death. I could only imagine as I sat back in my isolation room, how much of this is happening all day everyday as some succumb to this virus and do not make it. Truly sad and scary to think. Their loved ones and families may have called 911 just like what happened to me just under a week ago, and not have a chance to hug their loved ones or tell them they love them. Can you imagine if the last conversation with their loved one was a fight or an argument or of anger, then never got a chance to amend, or to say sorry, or make peace. Suddenly life happens and corona can hit you hard. You go out on emergency 911 ambulance call, they arrive and take you in within 5 minutes from the time you call. Which they did in my case, then you get taken away. Some may never have a chance to go back home to say I love you, I am sorry, or to hug their children, spouse or loved ones. When you are on that edge and you cannot breathe and gasping for air, you may ask God to give you one last chance to make amends or to say something to someone or make amends for what you may have held in you forever, be it a grudge or anger. Sometimes you ask God, please give me a chance to say to whoever… I love you. Forgive me. I am sorry. Or, yes I forgive you.

I am sitting here in isolation, with no oxygen, I believed and challenged God yesterday morning and took all those artificial tubes off, and have been breathing on my own since, and my levels of everything are normal today. No more headaches, no more joint pain, no more high temperatures.

I feel great. Thanking God for giving me the strength to sit and type this and thanking him for the opportunity to go back home to my wife and children, and as soon as I am cleared to have contact, have the opportunity to squeeze them and hug them so tight and long, tell them I love them. Every opportunity I get. We take these things for granted. Remember, tomorrow is not promised to anyone. Nothing is promised. NOTHING! **Proverbs 27:1 says—Do not boast about tomorrow, for you do not know what a day may bring.** Love without reservation, do not hold grudges or hate.**1 John 4:8—Whoever does not love does not know God, because God is love.** It is so not necessary or worth it to carry hate and anger. Do not leave the house upset on angry. Do not go to bed upset or angry. **Ephisians 4:26–31—"In your anger do not sin": Do not let the sun go down while you are still angry and do not give the devil a foothold. Anyone who has been stealing must steal no longer, but must work, doing something useful with their own hands, that they may have something useful with their own hands, that they may have something to share with those in need. Do not let any unwholesome talk come out of your mouths, but only what is helpful for building others up according to their needs, that it may benefit those who listen. Do not grieve the holy spirit of God, with whom you were sealed for the day of redemption. Get rid of all bitterness, rage and anger, brawling and slander, along with every form of malice.** Be at peace, love everyone, be happy, because you wake up every morning, be thankful for that. God woke you up, not your intelligence, not your job, not your money or business, not your wealth, but GOD. Remember that every day. We owe it all to him.

Do not be envious, do not be jealous. Be grateful. Remember to tell those you love that you love them. If you cannot say it or pride holds your tongue, at least show it.

You never know if God will grant you a chance to see your loved ones again, or even speak with them ever again.

I am so fortunate and blessed for God to be giving me a chance to live through this experience, and survive this deadly virus that is taking out hundreds of lives daily. As I get ready to be discharged, looking forward to my next chapter and the purpose God has for me. I want to take this opportunity to say. I love you all so dearly. May God continue to bless and protect you.

God has always showed up and said not now my son. I grant you more life. He has been so awesome and showed me he is protecting me and still wants me to be on this earth. Time and time again, over and over and over again. I am speechless. He is an amazing and faithful God, full of mercy. He has been good to me. I LOVE YOU GOD.

CHAPTER ONE

The Many Hats I Wear, My Path

I HAVE ALWAYS been a people person. I love to joke and see people laugh. I love people and humanity. I get this trait from my parents. My father has always been one who extended his hand to make sure the under privileged and needy were taken care of. I have witnessed him give and help so many people as I grew up, including family members. He was blessed to have a job and career that helped to put him in that position. My mother was the same, like any mother she had the interest of her 6 children and their wellbeing first before anything and made sure we all had everything we wanted. My parents would make sure we all went to church every Sunday, no excuses and no exceptions. As a little kid, I went through all the Sunday school and remember being in a few plays, acting roles and musicals at various stages over my early years. My parents had a tighter grip on me and made sure I attended church and some weekdays would go to midweek prayer services and church meetings with them. This was the case as a little boy before school age to my whole time in primary school. We lived in Hatfield, a suburb in Harare. Things changed when I completed primary school and went to high school. I applied to several high schools and was happy to learn when I was accepted at Prince Edward School in Belvedere Harare. This was and still remains one of the best high schools in the country. Both my elder brothers also attended there.

In high school I started playing more sport and engaged in extra activities. I played a lot of sport, basketball and rugby being the main two I excelled in, this took away my church schedule, weekends or weekday prayer services and Saturday plays or acting or activity rehearsals slowly get eliminated from my schedule.

I had to stay long hours at school for practice or weekend games against other schools and institutions. Prince Edward was a very prestigious school and it was a privilege to be in the institution. Over the years in high school I started becoming popular among my peers as an athlete and people person. I felt on top of the world and so empowered and felt like everyone loved me. As I completed my fourth year in high school. After taking the Cambridge "O" level exams, as I was home during the holidays, clearly I had drifted away from attending church and the few times I went to church with my parents, it felt different. I would see some of the people I used to go to Sunday school with some four or five years prior still engaged in the church and looked so comfortable and belonging. Some had taken roles as ushers or being involved in youth or other church groups. I somehow felt out of place and was now only going to church with my parents just so not to disappoint them. I did not have an excuse or reason not to attend. I could not say I have rugby practice today or we have a match. It would still feel awkward for me to be in the church setting, I somehow missed the school environment and being a popular recognized figure, being the man. Where everyone gravitated to me and I was one of the popular students at school. Being in church felt different. I remember a couple of the people from years prior, and some Sunday school members I attended with would come and talk to me with excitement and would happy to see me, but as much as I tried to fake the excitement I was cold not as welcoming, it sadly showed and I could not act that good. Maybe in the back of my mind felt guilty that I had drifted away from God. Or maybe I just felt I was on a better more fun path with being a popular student and enjoyed being revered by my peers at school more than the structured and laid back church life.

I did not have a spark or yearning to grow in Christ at this moment because I felt being the focus of attention and being the popular kid in school was more fun and exciting. I would reluctantly agree to go to church with my mom and dad along with Tendai, maybe a few more times that school holiday. My four other older siblings had moved out of the house, all married and starting their new lives. It was just me and my little sister at home then.

Weeks later, day one of my final two years in high school. During assembly, the headmaster Mr. Clive Barnes arguably the best headmaster Zimbabwe has ever had, announced seven students to be Prefects. A school prefect is a monitor or chosen student leaders who would help instil discipline and rules to other students and peers. Every year, seven or eight returning students would be chosen to be prefects, from this group, a Senior Prefect, deputy Headboy and Headboy of the school will be chosen the following final year in high school. These seven or eight prefects are famously known as legends.

Being chosen to be a legend on day one of my last two years in high school only made my head grow bigger. I felt like I was on top of the world, I would go on to continue to be a popular student, playing first team rugby (Tigers) and representing my province and at national level. I felt like I have reached my peak in life and I will never see bottom again. I will always be loved revered and will be popular forever. By this time I probably went to my parent's church maybe one more time in those two years. I felt I did not need church or God to be happy, I felt I had reached the top of the world by being the revered and loved athlete and legend. I rather be the popular legend and date any girl I wanted.

I met my wife for the first time in 1990 in the neighborhood I grew up in, I felt like she was the prettiest and most elegant girl I had seen. Though we only started dating six years after we first met. In my head, I said to myself, I will marry this girl one day. My first step of deep faith. This was way back before cell phones, it was one school holiday and I was fortunate after our conversation, we exchanged our home landline numbers. I would keep in touch and check on her periodically over the years. We were not dating but remained friends for the next several years. In my last year of high school, I must admit I had a few options to pick as a date for the end of year dinner dance. I was disappointed when she refused to be my date for my dinner dance. She refused to be my date stating she felt I had too many girlfriends. "How could she turn down a tiger, a legend?" I understand we were not dating at this time, however, but come on. I must admit. I was still disappointed by her decision. I thought to myself, many high school girls would jump for this opportunity and to be invited to an end of year prestigious dinner dance by a tiger legend. This was probably one of the first times I felt rejected by a girl I really liked. However, my second choice to the dance accepted the invitation so that ended well, I bring it up every so often and tell her she missed out on the best date and dinner dance.

After high school, I decided to prove myself to her and told her I was going to stop talking to or entertaining all the other girls. She agreed to go on dates with me a few times. We got closer and closer, we soon started dating. She landed a job at Air Zimbabwe, the national airline. The year after high school I got a referral from Mr. Barnes to work for satellite company (Ellies Electronics in Msasa Harare), a leading satellite company in the country and region at the time.

The company had been around for about three years and was continuing to expand and take a large market share. The satellite industry had just started booming in Zimbabwe. It was a great job that allowed me a good salary, company car and great benefits. I was happy and proud to get a large satellite dish at a staff discount, and had it installed at my parent's house in Hatfield, this allowed us to watch television from all over the world including USA, Europe, and other international networks. I purchased the largest package possible. To this day this first gift to my parents still looms as a feature at their home. I really enjoyed working for this company, meeting and exceeding marketing and sales targets. Again I felt nothing would ever go wrong, life was good.

Zimbabwe was known as the basket of Africa, at that point of my life I had everything I wanted. After a year of working for the satellite company I decided to take a vacation to visit USA, I had always wanted to travel to the states. Growing up I would always tell my mother I will go to America one day and I would periodically sing a song from a TV show to her. "I want to be an American. In the land of the free, in the land of the free. It's right for meee…" I forget the name of the TV show. All I envisioned as a kid was me moving to America. It could be the movies, TV shows, the fashion, the cars. Maybe it was the image and branding that the Americans have always been great at that got me hooked on America from a young age. I kept my mind on that vision.

In 1996 I decided to go to the American Embassy and apply for a visiting visa. I travelled to America and vacationed in Texas, Nebraska and Chicago. I really enjoyed my trip and on return to Zimbabwe decided to start applying to colleges in America to go back and study.

I was accepted at a few colleges, and I chose Bellevue University in Nebraska. I soon left Zimbabwe to go to college. By then, my relationship with Madelien had grown stronger and that was one thing that made me have reservations about leaving Zimbabwe for an extended time in college away from her. As an employee of Air Zimbabwe, she was able to get an employee 10% discount ticket to come and visit. She took advantage of the opportunity and visited with me. I realized then, this is the woman I want to spend the rest of my life with.

I studied business, management and accounting. I worked at Mutual of Omaha as a claims analyst. In year 2000, I moved to Baltimore Maryland. In2003, I went to nursing school and graduated in April of 2004, I did not wait to do the recommended review before sitting for the boards, I registered and sat for the boards, one week before Memorial weekend. This proved to be God pushing me to take the board exams before a major accident a week later during the Memorial weekend in 2004. I will elaborate this sentiment in chapter three. The same year 2004, I started a tax consulting and book keeping company in Baltimore Maryland, Double R Taxes, I have been operating these offices in Baltimore and have maintained this business and operation since 2004, to current. 2011 I took IT security classes and certifications in SAP Governance Risk and Compliance (GRC) and Security. I have worked for a few companies in IT security over the years including the federal division at Accenture, and continue to enjoy the industry and growth in this world of technology.

In 2019, I opened two more offices in Georgia, Decatur and Riverdale to expand my tax preparation and book keeping business, Infinity Financial Services LLC. I am also an Executive Director along With my long time friend, Godfrey J (Goofy), of Easylinx Logistix LLC, we supply construction and agriculture equipment in the east and southern Africa region and continue to expand our reach on the continent including other shipping, trucking, freight brokerage, global networking, and our new app in the development phase "Truck3r On Call" app, coming soon.

My new passion and joy is a company we started with three other friends, Bernard, Hilary and Tapuwa. We invested into the real estate space and started a company Bright Ventures Holding Company LLC, we are identifying properties that are in areas that have potential for growth, give them a facelift, fix and modernize the properties and sell them at a profit. I am enjoying this real estate space and pray to continue to grow and expand in it. It is my new passion. My other new vision and passion is a reimaging and rebranding of Africa, that Godfrey and I started, Africa's Trending Inc. The idea is to change the negative perception from the rest of the world about Africa, and rebrand and change the perception and ultimately increase investment opportunities and show the positive images and opportunities of the rich continent, including promoting artists in different genres from the continent, exposing and introducing them to the rest of the world. Just like I was wowed by America as a young kid. The world needs to see Africa from a different light and erase the negative perceptions. Image is everything.

I am currently enrolled at a renowned university completing my MBA program, I have three more courses to complete this achievement and milestone. I look forward to the day I do, by the time of this publication I should have achieved that.

I have worked in different industries, Satellite, Hotel, sales, cable technician for a major cable company, in health as a nurse where I remain as needed PRN employee, IT Security, Governance Risk and Compliance, I have am a board member of two logistics companies, owner and CEO of two Tax and accounting companies, Real estate investor and looking forward to building the real estate portfolio. I have also started unsuccessfully, an insurance company that never took off as expected, I also attempted a group home and assisted living but failed at it. With the failure and unsuccessful businesses and startups came with lessons that I learnt and helped me not make the same mistake.

The failures gave me lessons and ideas to not repeat the same mistakes and be successful. At times in life we rush for every situation that presents itself in front of you. Not every opportunity is meant for you. Sometime we have to wait on God, sometimes we have to be patient. Over the years I have learnt sometimes less is more. It is not necessarily a case of biting more than you can chew. Sometimes we over fill our plate with stuff we know we are not even going to eat. Same mentality that makes me say, less is more. When you over fill your plate you slow yourself down. Like greed, just taking in everything and not give yourself time to breathe, stream line and focus. I have learnt over the years, it is better to specialize in something, be great at it before you graduate to go onto the next task. Unlike running with two or three tasks and eventually not even complete any of the tasks because you are equally subtracting hours and energy from each. Complete one task and then start a new one.

I have made that mistake over the years of accepting roles or jobs while my plate is already full. That is a recipe for failure because something is going to be neglected or delayed and cause and unhappy customer or client. Finish a task or project well before you accept or embark on a new one. Give yourself time to slow down and smell the roses. This life can come at you fast. Live it and learn to cherish and enjoy the moments with all its lessons.

Out of all these hats and responsibilities. The one I enjoy most is being a great husband to my wife and a great father to my children. From gymnastics, ballet, soccer practice and weekend games. I equally enjoy attending these events as much as they enjoy me being there. The fact that their dad is there, gives them that extra bounce in their step and may make them play a little harder.

This may contribute to increased assists or higher scoring average. It is a win, win situation. I enjoy spending every possible moment I can with my children, taking them to practice, to games, their matches, bowling, playing tennis with together as a family or just playing scrabble or cards after dinner. I enjoy them and pray for their protection and am blessed to be able to see all their milestones.

My father with his busy schedule made sure he always made time for us and with us. I know how important and special that made me feel.

Especially when they both used to come and watch me play rugby in high school, it made me play with an extra umph and grind, It always gave me extra wings. For that reason I told myself I will do the same or even more for my children. I find the time and balance to make sure I at least support them and they see my presence in everything or as much as humanly possible. Taking time to go for a walk at the park, hiking at the mountains, teaching them how to play chess and enjoying board and card games. Weekly game night. At the same time give them their space and independence. I enjoy the conversations we have. That opens the chain of communication and for them to always remain comfortable with me and feel free to talk to me about any or everything and not fear me judging them or creating a drift. I enjoy and cherish every minute I spend with them, they will always be my babies.

CHAPTER TWO

Spiritual Healing

EVERY MORNING BEFORE my father left home for work, I would sit briefly with him at the dining room table as he had breakfast. As he got into the car to drive off to work, I would run ahead of him to the gate and open for him routinely to please and make sure he realized that I was a good, obedient boy. As soon as he drove off, I would run back to finish the breakfast egg sandwich or whatever meal would have been made for dad. I am pretty sure finishing his breakfast was one of the major reasons I would want to sit with him every morning. Just maybe, next to the bonding of course.

This was a routine start to the day, my father worked at the Reserve Bank of Zimbabwe at the time, and as a young little boy I always wanted to please my father and make sure I was on his good side. I learnt a lot of leadership qualities from my dad, discipline, honor, respect, cleanliness, hard work, perseverance, faith. He was voted to be Chairman of the PTA (Parent Teachers Association) at my primary school when Daisy was in 6th grade, I was in 4th grade and Tendai was in 1st grade, he remained chairman at the school until Tendai finished her last year in primary school. He remained loved and respected by the principal, staff and other members for his leadership, fairness, guidance and presentation over the years. He was a very stern, respected man. My siblings and I were super behaved in his presence, the opposite when it was just my mother around. Not disrespectful, but we would turn out and be loud, more playful and just care free. As a young child I would remember when we heard his diesel pickup truck drive down the street with its distinct roaring sound, we would rush to straighten up and get behaving, or either compete to rush and open the gate if we were outside close to the gate. When dad would walk in the room, we could have been all jumping on the couches and driving my mother crazy, as soon as he walked in, we would act all innocent and the noise and foolishness would suddenly turn into and calmness and decent behavior.

My mother was an industrious woman who always had some sort of small business at the house. We had gardeners and maids that helped her with her projects. I remember we always had chickens, rabbits and an ever green garden that always would have produce. Seeing my mother being hands on and so hardworking and being an equal partner to raise her 6 children for most of the day while my dad was at work, is something I will always raise my hat to her with respect. **Psalm 128:2 You shall eat the fruit of your labor of your hands, you shall be blessed, and it shall be well with you.**

This weekday morning, I believe I was in 5th grade, it was a routine morning during the school holidays. As my dad was getting served his breakfast, I got up out of my room and went to sit with him at the dining room table, as always I looked forward to him handing me half his egg or bacon sandwich with half the cup of his rich tea or coffee, I would look forward to that little pre breakfast before breakfast every weekday. Not recalling the real reason. Either way, it was a routine. This specific morning after he passed me his leftover sandwich and got up to leave. I in turn followed behind and ran to the gate to open for him and wave him goodbye as always. I ran back to the table to finish my rich creamy coffee and sandwich. As I sat on the table, to get ready to enjoy my pre breakfast snack, before I could even take a bite. I had the sharpest pain and most painful headache I ever had in my life at the point. My mother, Daisy and Tendai were in the girls bedroom. I screamed so loud in pain, and my sisters came out running to check on me. I was rigid and grabbing onto the table cloth with my teeth clenched, my mother followed behind them and asked me what the problem was. I remember mentioning my head was hurting so bad as I was squirming with pain continuing to grab on the table cloth with my eyes totally closed. I do not remember anything else from that moment until I woke up in the hospital bed, opened my eyes in a hospital room surrounded by my family. They had called the ambulance to come and take me to the hospital. They say it took three paramedics to unclench my fists from the table cloth and carry my rigid body into the ambulance which was parked outside the verandah. As soon as my dad got to work, he got the message about the emergency and that I was transferred to the hospital. This was before cell phones or voicemail, so a lot of communication was with land lines and office phones.

The doctors did x-rays and tests to figure out what was wrong, all results came back normal, my vitals were stable and they drew blood to check for any infection. The doctors kept telling my parents, they do not see anything wrong with me, my neck and shoulder imaging was in perfect position, I had not had any sports injuries, had I had a recent fall or anything that could possibly lead to the stiffness, neck and head pain. The answer was no. My neck kept getting stiff, my headache kept getting stronger and worse. It was so painful as if I had someone constantly beat me with a hammer right in the middle of my brain and forehead. I do not remember ever feeling pain like that in my life before, It was excruciating. The only relief to this neck pain was I would have family members rub my neck and massage me to ease the stiffness and pain on my neck.

I would feel like my neck was being twisted and I had no control over it. I distinctly remember my brother Godwin, my cousin Innocent, and cousin Wayne would take turns to massage my neck and shoulder, Wayne was about 6 years my senior, and was a tall strong and muscular rugby player. I would feel so much relief when he massaged my shoulder and neck. I hoped visit hours would never end and that he rubbed and massaged my neck and shoulders all day.

The pain medications they were giving me in the hospital were not helping, the muscle relaxants and cream they applied to my neck and shoulder would not help, probably made it worse or the same. Only the massages did it for me. Next day visit hours did not come fast enough. I would look at the clock and start counting down the hours to the next day visiting hours so a family member could massage my stiff painful neck. After day 5 in the hospital with no improvement and no medical diagnosis or any treatment that showed signs of healing. I hear, my brothers Paul and Godwin, and other family members convinced my parents to have me discharged and try other means of getting me some help.

Faith and the Power of Healing

The medical and scientific option was clearly not working. My mother and aunts were not comfortable to take me to any traditional healers or any individual who practiced along those spiritual lines. They wanted only medical intervention along with the prayers for healing she would have with other family and church members. At this point, my condition had drastically declined. I was not eating, and had visibly lost weight, I was frail and hardly speaking. Ultimately my brother Paul convinced my parents to have me discharged and we try other means of treatment. I was feeble and unable to walk on my own. Research had been done for me to visit this lady prophet in a city in the west of Harare, Tynwild. We arrived at this prophet's residence. I was helped out of the car and propped to walk into the room with both my brothers on either side because I was too weak to walk on my own.

There was a line of people waiting outside, waiting to meet with the prophet, but for some reason I think in hind sight, my condition was the most critical and needed more immediate attention. We jumped the line and I was taken straight into this room where everyone outside was in line to go into and visit with. My eyes were still shut from the banging headache, and opening my eyes would bring light to my eyes and only intensify my headache, I would only minimally open them and squint them open just to have an idea where I was stepping and to help not just be dead weight to Paul and Godwin as they directed me into this room. "Sit him right there on the floor." The prophet said to my brothers.

I was shocked there was no couch or chair for me to sit on. I quickly opened my eyes to see who is saying this and a quick visual of the room and why I should be made to sit on the floor? The prophet was a woman. In my head I was anticipating to see a man for some reason. She was wearing this white coat and had a thick white belt of cloth material tied to the front of her waist.

The room hardly had any furniture except a couple of benches she had on the opposite side of the room I was sitting on. There was a little fire pit in the middle of the room which I eventually found out had a pot of porridge in it.

The prophet walked towards me and as both my brothers stood beside me on either side. My father who was driving a different vehicle and soon walked into the room behind us. The lady prophet asked my brothers to let me go and not support me. She held my head as I was in this weak state about to fall backwards on the floor. I remember she started praying and continued to hold my head to prevent me from falling. "Devil, I command you to leave, buda! Buda! devil buda! You do not belong here, I tremble you in the name of Jesus.

You have no power. Out! Out! Out!" Her voice kept getting louder and louder, as she prayed over me and declared my victory. (Buda! is my Zimbabwean language shona word which means "out!" I do not recall how long her prayer went on for, all I remember is the more she kept praying, I felt the stiffness in my pain go away, my muscles started relaxing, the headache subsided and by the time she said Amen. I was able to fully open my eyes and not feel and headache or pain. I was in shock, I could fully open my eyes and not intensify the headache. The headache was gone. She let go off my head and to the surprise of everyone in the room. I was able to sit up on my own with no support. The prophet walked to the middle of the room and opened the lid to the pot on the little fire, she poured some porridge in a wooden basin and walked back towards me and said to me. "You have not eaten in days, eat all this porridge and go home and resume your life. It is well." My appetite was back, as I sat on the floor and finished every drop of porridge in that bowl. I felt brand new, I was so happy and grateful and wished my dad will pay her as much as he possibly could because I felt she clearly saved my life. We may have been in the room for a total of 30 minutes, as my brothers attempted to hold me back up to stand and walk me back to the car, the lady prophet told them to let me go and I will be able to walk back in the car on my own strength. They obliged, and surely I had the strength to walk on my own. My father stayed behind in the room briefly I guess to thank the woman of God or pay her, he later stated she told him. If we had not gotten to her or a powerful person of God within that day, I may not have lived another 24 hours. The devil was out to destroy and take your son away.

John 10:10 ESV. The thief comes only to steal and kill and destroy. I came that they may have life and have it abundantly.

I never understood the spiritual, dark world or evil spirits and why some people like to see evil or have hate, are envious or just have devil tendencies and believe in evil spirits. As a little boy, up to today. I honestly don't get it. Love trounces hate any day, I believe love trumps hate.

Peter 4:8 NIV. Above all, keep loving one another earnestly, since love covers a multitude of sins.

Proverbs 3:3–4 NIV. Let love and faithfulness never leave you, bind them around your neck, write them on the tablet of your heart. Then you will win favor and a good name in the sight of God and man.

My dad, brothers and I drove back home were my mother, her sister Mai Mawoyo, my sisters, Choice, Daisy and Tendai were home waiting for me not knowing what to expect or how things will go, they were all in prayer mode. Everyone was in shock when we got home and I walked out of the car on my own strength and walked into the house without any support or anyone propping me up. My mother and her sister started crying out and praising God, thanking him for saving me. **John 14:13 ESV. Whatever you ask in my name, this I will do, that the father may be glorified in the son.** My mother has always been a prayer warrior and prays for all her children and family, all the time. I know this because we would have prayers every night and she would mention every one of her children by name and pray for all of us including her marriage with my father, until the present day, their praying tradition has never changed. Every night it was automatic that we would all congregate and pray individually, thankful for everything. As I went to the living room to sit and recoup, and be happy to be back home, everyone remained excited and could not believe the turnaround from being lethargic, frail and barely able to speak three hours prior, to now seeing me able to walk on my own, and have power to speak and respond to them without any difficulty.

It was the most exciting thing to everyone. I was served with food maybe half an hour after arriving home, and for years after that serving, Tendai and Daisy would make fun of how I cleaned the plate and ate that food like someone who had never seen food in their life. Indeed, I really chowed that meal, I destroyed it so fast.

To my defense, I really had not had a meal in almost 6 days. That was the beginning of my healing process and I clearly was ever so grateful to the lady prophet in Tynwild who I believe saved my life, prayed for me and made the pain go away. **Exodus 23:25 NIV. Worship the Lord your God, and his blessings will be on your food and water. I will take away sickness from among you.** It was the first time as a young boy I remember ever being around a prophet or had one pray for me.

As a toddler, my parents tell me all the time. I was about 9 months old, if I say the year I will tell my age. However, the family lived in the city of Rusape in Zimbabwe. 6 months before my dad joined the Reserve Bank he worked for Zimbabwe Republic Police for 5 years. There was a baby competition that would be held every year in the city that would include police and government personnel, school teachers and district workers.

The winner would be based on showing signs of good health and best looking baby. They tell me I won that competition and people in the neighborhood, police department and camp had no doubt I would win because I was so healthy and good looking. They nicknamed me Keke, (Cake). I am proud to say those good looks have never left from way back then when I won the competition and prize.

My parents say when they got home and were getting ready for bed, they kept hearing cats surrounding the house and mewing. It was the most weird thing to them and they distinctly remember that night because several kids (families) entered in the competition, it disappointed a lot of people that I won. To date they do not know who may have been involved in the most bizarre incident, but the cats stayed and made noise all night that night.

When my dad went out of the house and chase them away which he did, as soon as he walked back into the house, he started feeling ill, simultaneously I started crying nonstop and was very irritable. Like I stated earlier. My parents, family is a Christian believing family and do not believe in voodoo or evil spirits or witch doctors or witchcraft. However this night, they say was different. In the morning we both were feeling worse and sicker, we were both taken to Rusape General Hospital. For my dad, it was high fever and feeling dizzy. He even remembers the Dr who treated him to this day, Dr Irene, a European doctor at the hospital who gave him medication and something to induce him to throw up, he stated we had some kind of poisoning and had to induce vomiting. The same treatment was done for me. After we both through up immensely, we felt better and were both discharged after 1 day. My mother on the other hand stated was nonstop on a prayer mission praying for our healing and recovery. My parents are both convinced this incident all spiraled with haters and evil people who were not happy with me having won that health and beauty contest. The fact that I won both prizes did not sit well with some residents and city workers, how could the same family with both prestigious prizes?

Upsetting those who had put a lot of energy into winning this completion. The screaming cats all night around the house and by their bedroom window is what led them to that assumption and superstition to this day.

They thought that this was an evil spiritual spell that was cast by a jealous individual. I was 9 months old and clearly can only state what I was told about the sickness and brief hospitalization. My positive takeaway from this story they tell me is my good looks and nickname I got to be known by, Keke. The other spiritual, voodoo, dark side magic, I will not entertain or feed. I may end up following the energy into a negative darkness or hole. I choose life, I choose happiness, I choose positive energy, I choose to follow the teachings of Jesus. I choose love. Faith over fear. **Luke 10:19 NIV—Behold, I have given you authority to tread upon serpents and scorpions, and over all the power of the enemy. Nothing will harm you.**

The mind is a powerful thing, what we feed and grow in our thoughts and mind can affect us negatively if the thoughts are negative. They can affect us positively, if our thoughts are positive. Let us use our mind and brain to have positive and healthy thoughts. Feed and grow that energy, it only leads to positive energy and good will follow, the opposite is true. I deeply believe this and have found in my life when I tell myself and believe in something and put my might and energy into it and focus. More often than not, it aligns just as my thoughts and mindset takes me. **Whether you think you can, or you think you can't, either way you are right. (Henry Ford).** Indeed, the mind is a powerful thing. This idea and belief I elaborate and show to work in chapter six.

Ephesians 4:31–32 ESV. Let all bitterness and wrath and anger and clamor and slander be put away from you, along with all malice. Be kind to one another, tenderhearted, forgiving one another, as God in Christ forgave you.

Philipians 4:8 ESV. Finally brothers, whatever is true, whatever is honorable, whatever is just, whatever is pure, whatever is lovely, whatever is commendable, if there is any excellence, if there is anything worth of praise, think about these things.

CHAPTER THREE

Surviving Out of a Coma

MEMORIAL WEEKEND 2004. Myself and a group of close friends had set up and planned to go to Myrtle Beach South Carolina for the (Bike Fest) Bikers Weekend. This was a popular annual event that many bikers and people would just congregate, go to the beaches, ride bikes, socialize and have good times, bar hopping and just catching up with friends. We set up to travel as a group of about 7 friends. We went to get a rental pickup truck so we can load the two bikes we were taking with us to the bike fest, one which belonged to Wallen, one of my closest friends, and another owned by Derrick. We got all our supplies, cooler boxes, ice, beer, liquor and snacks to go. We prepared to have a fun filled exciting and merry weekend.

The road trip was as expected, fun and full of several stops to use the rest rooms and just stop and stretch. We left Baltimore early, about 8:00am. This was so we would arrive in the daytime and start with the festivities, hit the ground running. It is an 8hour drive from Baltimore to Myrtle Beach. Non of us wanted to drive the whole way, we kept changing drivers after a couple of hours. I drove the first 2 hours because I wanted to relax and enjoy my drink the rest of the way, so I took the first driving shift. Eventually we arrived at the hotel. I was feeling nice and tipsy with the drinks I had been having throughout the trip. We registered and checked in. As we offloaded our luggage and put our luggage in our rooms. I remember coming back to the truck and offloading the bikes, after I had put my luggage in my room. The last thing on the agenda was to offload the bikes off the truck. South Carolina does not have a universal helmet law.

So as we offload the bikes, we are seeing all these bikers and riders having good times, the roaring sounds of bikes gave that thrilling and exhilarating feeling. As soon as we offloaded the bikes, in my shorts and flip flops, I rushed to Wallen and said to him. "Give me the bike keys." He was like, "Jose, why the rush. Let us ride later." We all call each other Jose by the way, a handful of us call each other Jose. My adrenaline rush was high, we went back and forth about him giving me the keys to take a quick ride around the block and quickly get acquainted to the festivities.

I guess I won that exchange. I got the keys from him, got on the bike, turned on the ignition, revved the bike to match what was happening around us and to express the Baltimore crew had arrived. I took my foot off the clutch, I turned around in the parking lot to get onto the street. As I did this, I accelerated too hard. In my head I want to show my skill and do a wheelie (When one rides on the back wheel alone) and show off my skills, and then return to park the bike. **Jeremiah 9:23 NIV. Thus says the Lord: Let not the wise man boast in his wisdom, let not the mighty man boast in his might, let not the rich man boast in his riches.** Showing off is not a good thing. Do not boast or try to show you are more accomplished and important, have more bling or better assets or material. I learnt the hard way. Be humble.

In hind sight, I have no idea why I decided to show that I have a bigger, better, faster bike and am better than. "my bike is bigger, better and louder than yours mentality". **James 4:16–17 But now you boast and brag, and all such boasting is evil. It is a sin when someone knows the right thing to do and doesn't do it.** As I accelerated at such a top speed, before I knew it, I lost control, the bike swerved off and I went and hit a light pole at a ferocious speed. As stated earlier, I was not wearing a helmet when my head hit the pole. I instantly passed out and as I lay on the ground motionless with no sign of life.

Wallen tells me the guys all rushed to me and realized instantly this was a disaster. I was unconscious and lay lifeless on the pavement. None of the guys had medical background or knew what to do. Wallen called 911, because of the congestion on the streets and crowds, the quickest and best mode was for them to send a helicopter, waiting for an ambulance and taking me to the nearest hospital in that state would have made me lose valuable time to be revived and saved. The helicopter arrived and air lifted me to the nearest trauma center.

I lay motionless in ICU for three days in a coma. Intubated and receiving oxygen, and connected to life support machinery. I had blood clots in my brain, broken right clavicle, damage brachial plexus nerves. A few months prior, I had had a contentious discussion with Madelien about the importance of having health insurance. I was for the argument that we have been wasting a lot of money and insurance was not important. I am glad she won that argument. I tried and failed to convince her that we cancel our health insurance. In hind sight, we apparently had a great policy that was able to cover majority of all medical cost and treatments. Without insurance I do not know if I would have been able to get air lifted or the care I ended up receiving. Sad to note, but I believe when you do not have insurance, they do the bare minimum. I thank God I was able to get excellent care I received.

I am glad you won the insurance argument Madelien. It may have saved me and insured I got the best care and facilities possible, including the rehabilitation that ensued. **Ecclesiastes 7:12 ESV. For the protection of wisdom is like the protection of money, and the advantage of knowledge is that wisdom preserves the life of him who has it.**

That memorial weekend we had planned to be an exciting fun filled weekend. Ended up being a disastrous weekend. Wallen had to call Madelien when the incident happened, who in turn informed my mother and father. The doctors at the time informed my family that, if I came out of the coma, I would be a cabbage, and not have my motor skills anymore. They informed my family that I probably be wheelchair bound or not be able to do much on my own. On the third day in this comatose state, I was able to move my extremities. I opened my eyes for the first time. This was my first step to recovery. **Ephisians 2:8 For by grace you have been saved through faith. And this is not your own doing; it is the gift of God.**

Friday, Saturday, Sunday. The weekend we were all looking forward to, did not happen anyway close to what was planned. The friends I travelled with, namely, Wallen, Godfrey, Derrick spent a lot of their time in traveling to visit with me in hospital instead. A lot of travelers returned back to their respective cities, we had planned to drive back to Baltimore on Memorial day Monday afternoon. Which is the day I first made body movement. I started to be able to move my extremities more in bed. By Tuesday, Wallen who stayed at the hospital with me had to figure out how to get me transported to a hospital in Baltimore. This was so he could go back to work, and have me at a close hospital to Madelien, Daisy and my friends. We did not have any friends or family in South Carolina, transferring me to Baltimore was the best option. Being eight hours away from everyone I knew was not an option. The doctors and therapists agreed for the transfer on the Wedneday after I had gained a little more consciousness and stability. The doctors and therapists suggested we took frequent breaks and should definitely drive to any medical facility if I started having pain or needed oxygen or any medical attention at any time during the drive. Wallen signed off and assured the doctors we would be fine.

Wednesday afternoon I was wheeled in a wheelchair, transferred by two assist into the reclined passenger seat. They had me stabilized and medicated for pain, along with a fentanyl patch to help with my shoulder pain which I later realized I am allergic to. I would hallucinate and talk about imaginary doctors and incidents whenever this patch was on me. No one ever understood the hallucinations and loose association talk until it was traced that I would only act this way after I got that pain patch applied to me.

It was a long road trip and I would feel every turn, bump or uneven road after the sedation medication wore off. The pain would intensify through my body throughout that road trip. The pain medicine would help the pain subside for a couple of hours at a time. I had general aches and body pain, including shoulder pain the whole trip, but being that it was the best decision to have me close to my friends and family was a no brainer. I had to endure the road trip and drive back to Baltimore. I am not sure if flying was an option we considered, but all I know Wallen stated he had to get back to his job in Baltimore. He had no more available paid time off hours, and was in no way going to leave me with no friends or family in Myrtle Beach.

By 2004, my sister Daisy had moved to Baltimore with Madelien and me. She had come from Zimbabwe after she had lost her husband four years earlier in a car accident. We lived on the 3rd floor in an apartment in Cockeysville, Wallen lived two blocks away from us on the main level and there was no need for stair climbing. I spent the night at his place in their guest room after being helped out of the vehicle and transferred by 3 people and helped to walk into the room I spent the night.

The following morning after arriving in Baltimore from the road trip, my pain was not subsided and my shoulder really needed attention. I was hallucinating and continued to be lethargic. Madelien and Daisy were happy to have me back in Baltimore, but clearly worried and deeply concerned about my condition. 911 was called and I was put on a stretcher and transferred to a renowned hospital in Baltimore Maryland, where I was admitted for another four weeks. I had to learn how to walk, I had to learn how to talk, my speech was slurred and I would use word salad and not make sense. I had to learn the alphabet and how to write my name again. I had memory loss and definitely my short term memory was affected. The head injury I had suffered on the bike accident and blood clots in my brain were the result of this forgetfulness and almost total loss of memory. I would get frustrated after being told a simple sentence or sequence or 3 numbers and when asked to repeat, I would be blank and not remember anything. This went on for a couple of weeks until I slowly started to recall things again. I kept fighting and wanting to improve and get better. I would like to prove to my therapists that I am improving. My motivation was to improve and get myself better and show signs of improvement to them so they could get me discharged. My memory was so bad I had forgotten my own siblings and family members. I remember one evening Paul called me from South Africa to check in me and find out how my recovery was. I told him I did not know who he was. "I have no brothers, I do not know you." I told him. He had to tell me who he was and eventually after telling me who I was and narrating my story to me I slowly remembered, and started to make sense of who was who and remembering people, it was a really difficult and sad phase of my life, I almost lost all my memory. Over time my memory began improving. The different therapy and rehabilitation activities helped me improve greatly. Learning to write my name was painful to do but it all eventually came back. Yes, the word was if I survived the coma. I would be a cabbage, good for nothing and incapable of doing anything for myself. **Proverbs 16:1 (CEV). We humans make plans, but the Lord has the final word. Matthew 19:26 But Jesus beheld and said unto them, with men this is impossible; but with God all things are possible.**

I refused to remain in that state and believed I would improve. The power of thought and seeing myself healed and on the other side. The mind is a powerful thing indeed.

Believing I will walk with no support or walker again, I will speak with no slur, my memory will come back. Thanking God for healing and restoration was my daily portion. I had to see the victory and receive it. **Mark 11:24 Therefore I tell you, whatever you ask for in prayer, believe that you have received it, and it will be yours.** Sometimes we do not see it or understand how it will happen, but we just have to believe. That I did, and I recommend you change your mindset and receive it as you pray and declare that healing or whatever it is you are seeking from God.

Be obedient, believe it and receive it. **John 7:38 Whoever believes in me, as Scripture has said, rivers of living water will flow from within them.** My mother arrived in Baltimore from Zimbabwe to be with me during this time, we had been through the coma phase, the statement that, "I would be a cabbage if I made it." Frightened everyone my family and everyone who knew and cared for me.

I was happy to have my mother around. I remember crying like I never cried before one afternoon when I was sitting with her in outr apartment in Baltimore. In my slurred speech, narrating to her how the past 4 weeks had been. We both cried when I expressed how God saved me and gave me another chance. A week later I was scheduled to meet with the surgeon who was going to do the final CT scans before they schedule my 2 operations. One to fix my clavicle and connect my brachial plexus nerves, these are nerves that helps one able to raise their arm up and down and above their shoulder. My right arm was dead and I did not have feeling in it. The other operation the surgeon had anticipated and planned to do was to do with the blood clots in my head and brain and figure how best to resolve that problem.

On the day of the appointment with the doctor and surgeon, I went with my mother. I had the CT scans done and x-rays of my shoulder and clavicle, to confirm the diagnosis and schedule the operations. To the surprise of the surgeon, my mother and myself. The blood clots in my brain had disappeared, the clavicle had realigned itself and my nerves had regenerated and began to grow and connect on their own. The two potential surgeries I was meant to get to repair and reconnect my clavicle had to be cancelled.

It may seem like a fictional movie, but the surgeon declared this was rare to ever happen. A week prior, there was reason to operate, and on that particular day, surgery was not an option. God operated me in my sleep is what I would tell my family and friends after that incident. I am glad to state that my right hand fully recovered, I am able to move and raise my right hand and arm in any direction with no restrictions, reservation or pain. God truly did this for me. I have 100% full use of both my hands, arms and can raise my right hand functionally except for limitation on my golf swing but I am overjoyed and grateful that I still able to do as I please with both hands and arms, write, lift my children, nieces and nephews, play sports, basketball, bowling, or whatever I may choose. My memory is 100% back. **Jeremiah 30:17 But I will restore you to health and heal your wounds, declares the Lord.**

I would have several friends, workmates, college classmates and neighbors come and visit me in hospital. I felt the love and the encouragement.

Four weeks after my initial admission, I was discharged with follow up physical and speech therapy which I would continue for another month.

I went through a rigorous rehabilitation and treatment plan which I thank God I was able to improve and fully recover. **Jeremiah 33:6 Nevertheless, I will bring health and healing to it, I will heal my people and will let them enjoy abundant peace and security.**

The reason I took the nursing boards one week after graduation and decided not to join everyone else in review classes and study groups was not because I felt more intelligent or more ready. It was God preparing me for the journey because he knew what was to come.

My close friends and family questioned my decision and tried to talk me into delaying, but I just had a conviction to register and take the board exams that week. 10 days later was the Memorial Holiday trip which landed me in a coma, and when I got out of the coma, doctors presumptive assessments was I was going to be a cabbage, or wheelchair bound.

God knew I could not sit for any board exam in my state and for the next couple of months with my health and mental status. When I was home after discharge from hospital the next few weeks we mentally unstable and painful. Thinking I was this young, vibrant and full of life individual who could just get up and go wherever and whenever I pleased, playing basketball, tennis, going to the gym, movies, bars, clubs, sports games, concerts, events. Just living my best life and enjoying being out there in the world. God allowed these stumbles in my life for a reason, for me to realize his power and worth. Church or God was not on top of my list, I hardly made time to think of God and his mercies, the only times I would pray was during meals while saying a short grace. A tradition that has stayed with me since high school. It had been years since I set foot in a church at this point and at the time of my accident.

I truly was not religious or member of any church or at least attend one for that matter. I was slowly getting into depression. Crying at night or whenever I was alone was not uncommon. "God, why me?" I would ask. I asked this question in front of my mother one afternoon as I sat in a recliner chair in the living room with tears running down my cheeks.

She came and sat next to me and said. "But who? Who would you sit here and point to and say God, put that person in the situation I am in, heal me instead." This statement sobered me up. She was making me realize God does not make mistakes and in the moment giving me tough love. Telling me to keep the faith and believe you will get healed. No one on this earth deserves to be sick, crippled, ill or paralyzed. We are all God's children, asking why me is like saying to God, allow it to happen to other people and not me. We are all created equal and no one deserves more pain than the other. Remember the devil came to steal, kill and destroy. He is the one we have to conquer and fight. He is the enemy. **John 10:10 The thief comes only to steal and kill and destroy. I came that they may have life and have it abundantly.** "We have to stay steadfast and resolute in the Lord and pray for healing, while we keep the faith and believe he will do it for us. God is able my son, do not ask God why me, thank him instead that he saved you and brought you this far. God is good, God is love. He wants the best for us and wants us to live in his love and abundance. Trust in the Lord. No one deserves the pain and suffering. Just receive the healing, ask for complete restoration and do not look back or question God? **Jermiah 30:17 ESV. For I will restore health to you, and your wounds I will heal, declares the Lord.** "Tell me a name or a person who you feel right now should be in the position or state you are in?" I remember this conversation from my mother like it was 10 minutes ago. It was so sobering and helped me kick out of the pity party and depression mode I was slowly getting into. That five minute conversation alone was so powerful to me and made me look at the whole picture different.

I started believing again and told myself I will get through this. "I need to be grateful, I need to trust God and believe he has plans to heal me. I need to keep the faith and know him more, I need to pray more and get closer to God."

My driving privileges had been taken away until I had a clearance from my doctor. I had short term memory loss that frustrated me so much as I would forget the simplest and most basic things. I would ask repetitive questions on stuff and topics I had just discussed, this I am sure frustrated all the people who were unfortunate to experience this repetitive questioning, but is frustrated me more.

I did not know if I would get back to normal or if my memory would come back. The doctors and therapists told me, it will take time, there is no time frame, some people fully recover within a couple of months, some in 6 months, some may never recover. There is no telling, but just keep being optimistic and engaging with people, looking at old pictures, reading old emails, old notes and school materials, engaging family and asking as much as your brain can absorb, do not put pressure on yourself. Hopefully, eventually it will all come back together.

By the second week of July, I was eager to start driving and being more independent. As I continued to go through therapy and doing better with my memory exercises, it gave me confidence that I was on track to healing and recovery. I would eventually get cleared to start driving towards the end of the month and my memory was a lot better.

The first few times I had to be supervised by another licensed driver, so Madelien or Daisy would accompany me to make sure I remembered how to and my way around. My mother would not be the best choice for this clearance test because in Zimbabwe like most places in the world, they drive on the left side of the road, and this would confuse us both and make a recipe for another disaster, so we left the driving reorientation to Madelien and Daisy. Mother was not too familiar with the area as well, Google maps was not a thing, so we decided to stick to that plan.

On more than two occasions when I was now driving on my own around this period, I remember calling Madelien or Daisy to inform them of the intersection I was on, and ask them to direct me to get home. These couple of incidents had them and myself worried that I was relapsing and not improving. Soon I was back on track and remembering my way around like nothing ever happened. All was well. I am able to walk steady, my right hand is almost fully functional and I am able to raise it, my speech is no longer slurred. One afternoon after lunch as I sat in front of the computer going through my nursing program notes, reviewing the syllabus, review-ing medications, and their side effects, as I was getting ready to resume work in the field of study I went to school for and sacrificed so much to achieve. A song started playing on radio from a then very popular R&B musician, "You saved me." It hit me so hard and I started crying and sob-bing Like I had never cried before, my mother yet again who was practi-cally with me 75% of the time during these couple of months as Madelien and Daisy had started working, we would spend the whole day together talking and getting some motherly care and therapy. She came and sat next to me and I could see she tried to hold her tears, but she started crying as well, I leaned on her shoulder. I remember we both cried and sobbed as the whole song played to the end.

I guess from her perspective, God had given her son another life line and had truly saved me from death. We both continued to cry so hard together as she tried to comfort me at the same time realize what I had gone through the past couple of months. Nothing but God. He saved me. He truly did, there is no other explanation of the miraculous healings and great recovery we both acknowledged and realized, and it did not need anyone to tell us this, our spirit and emotions knew exactly why we sobbed in that moment.

Ephesians 2:8–9 For by grace you have been saved through faith. And this is not your own doing, it is the gift of God, not a result of your works, so that no one may boast.

Indeed I had great medical care, nurses, doctors and therapists to go through all my phases of recovery and healing. God is truly good to me. After sobbing and crying for as long as the song played and minutes after. I remember my mother saying, Now that you are able to go up and about, we need to go to church this weekend and thank God for your healing and give him honor and praise. I will talk with Madelien and Daisy to see which church we can start attending.

Mother was going to be with us for like 3 more weeks before she travelled back to Zimbabwe. She had been with me the majority of the time through my recovery and I will always cherish the sacrifice she made to spend 3 months away from her home to be with her little boy. Encourage me, motivate me, let me see light at the end of the tunnel, remove fear, helped rebuild my faith, made sure we were plugged back into the church become regular attendees again, and made sure I was back on my feet. I appreciate you Midhu, your love and support is never ending. I love you always.

After mom left to go back to Zimbabwe, we remained regular members at one of the churches we had started attending. Empowerment Temple, led by Pastor Jamal Bryant. A very gifted and powerful preacher in my opinion. He moves and captivates in a way that is not common. Mostly on all the weekends that we did not have to work, we made sure we attended church, we all looked forward to his teachings and the word. We kept attending until we moved to Atlanta in 2007.

Psalm 46:10 ESV. Be still and know that I am God.

Hebrews 11:1 Now faith is the assurance of things hoped for, the conviction of things not seen.

Hebrews 11:6 ESV. And without faith it is impossible to please God, because anyone who comes to him must believe that he exists and that he rewards those who earnestly seek him.

CHAPTER FOUR

My Covid-19 Story. Surviving the Coronavirus...

Why is the disease being called coronavirus disease 2019, COVID-19

On February 11, 2020 the World Health Organization announced an official name for the disease that is causing the 2019 novel coronavirus disease 2019, "CO" stand for "corona", "VI" for "virus," and "D" for disease. Formerly this disease was referred to as "2019 novel coronavirus" or "2019-nCoV". The most common symptoms are fever, coughing and shortness of breath or difficulty breathing, sore throat, some symptoms include head ache, joint pain, fatigue, chills—sometimes shaking, loss of taste or smell. Symptoms can be mild or severe and may appear 2–14 days after exposure to the virus. Reference: https://www.cdc.gov/

How Does Coronavirus Attack Your Body?

A *virus* infects your body by entering healthy cells. There, the invader makes copies of itself and multiplies throughout your body.

The new coronavirus latches its spiky surface proteins to receptors on healthy cells, especially those in your lungs.

Specifically, the viral proteins bust into cells through ACE2 receptors. Once inside, the coronavirus hijacks healthy cells and takes command. Eventually, it kills some of the healthy cells.

How Does Coronavirus Move Through Your Body?

COVID-19, the illness caused by the coronavirus, starts with droplets from an infected person's cough, sneeze, or breath. They could be in the air or on a surface that you touch before touching your eyes, nose, or mouth. That gives the virus a passage to the mucous membranes in your throat. Within 2 to 14 days, your immune system may respond with symptoms may include but not limited to: Fever, coughing, difficulty breathing, headache, fatigue, joint pain, loss off smell, loss of taste.

The virus moves down your respiratory tract. That's the airway that includes your mouth, nose, throat, and lungs. Your lower airways have more ACE2 receptors than the rest of your respiratory tract. So COVID-19 is more likely to go deeper than viruses like the *common cold*.

Your lungs might become inflamed, making it tough for you to breathe. This can lead to pneumonia, an infection of the tiny air sacs (called alveoli) inside your lungs where your blood exchanges oxygen and carbon dioxide.

If your doctor does a CT scan of your chest, they'll probably see shadows or patchy areas called "ground-glass opacity."

For most people, the symptoms end with a cough and a fever. More than 8 in 10 cases are mild. But for some, the infection gets more severe. About 5 to 8 days after symptoms begin, they have shortness of breath (known as dyspnea). Acute respiratory distress syndrome (ARDS) begins a few days later.

ARDS can cause rapid breathing, a fast heart rate, dizziness, and sweating. It damages the tissues and blood vessels in your alveoli, causing debris to collect inside them. This makes it harder or even impossible for you to breathe.

Many people who get ARDS need help breathing from a machine called a ventilator.

As fluid collects in your lungs, they carry less oxygen to your blood. That means your blood may not supply your organs with enough oxygen to survive. This can cause your kidneys, lungs, and liver to shut down and stop working.

Not everyone who has COVID-19 has these serious complications. And not everyone needs medical care. But if your symptoms include trouble breathing, get help right away for this may be fatal and lead to death.

Reference: https://www.webmd.com/lung/coronavirus-covid-19-affects-body

The virus had started spreading around the world in a scary way. I remember having conversations with a lot of my family, most who are still in Zimbabwe and South Africa, how they needed to stay safe. I would call my parents to give them all the knowledge I had of the new virus and to make sure they stayed safe.

Teaching of the social distancing, hand washing and to stop receiving guests and visitors at the house. I told them to lock the gates and not shake hands with people or strangers. My parents have a lot of people visit them at their home, be it people from their church, neighborhood friends, or customers who may come to purchase something from my mother's evergreen garden, vegetables or fruit. They also have a grinding mill, liqour store, butchery and supermarket and a bar lounge in Chitungwiza which is 30 minutes drive from the house. For this reason and the fact that they are both older and considered vulnerable population. It worried me greatly to think they were in constant contact with friends, customers and patrons. We all decided as siblings to suggest they shut down the business and the operations to avoid them having much human contact.

This decision was not taken lightly by both of them as they have always been active and had that keeping them busy and occupied. They reluctantly agreed to isolate at home and as we figure out even after this pandemic passes and life gets back to normal, for them to rent out the operations and just fully retire. Will be hard to convince them, but that is the plan. My cousin Taka who now resides in Melbourne Australia would share the same sentiments with me when we spoke, about how we need to keep reiterating to our aging parents, the importance of avoiding contracting the virus and to educate them on best practices and what to avoid. Fortunately it was not a hard task to convince them about the social distancing or the importance of it, because by now they were seeing the alarming deaths and how the virus was affecting several countries in Europe, America and in China were most research point it as were it was first identified in wholesale food market in Wuhan China.

One morning in mid April I got a call from Daisy, she also lives in Melbourne Australia with her husband Munya. She was audibly upset as I calmly answered her call. "I am so mad" she said, "I called home and found out that dad while driving from the family farm in Wedza, stopped and gave a hitch hiker a lift and drove with him all the way to Harare. How can he be so reckless? I called him and gave him a piece of my mind." She went on to express how she reiterated to him the importance of not travelling and avoiding giving people rides. You do not know who you are carrying, if they have the virus or have been exposed to it. Putting yourself at risk while driving that long drive maybe with windows closed.

She told me by the end of the conversation, he truly understood the importance of this and promised her he would not do it again. Daisy was more upset that if the stranger had been exposed to the virus and transfers it to my dad in the air particles due to their proximity and long drive, then get home and expose mom, and Rutendo (Daisy's daughter) who resides at home with mom and dad. The thought of the whole family catching the corona virus because dad felt sorry for a stranger and decided to give him a ride, traumatized Daisy and she definitely had a valid point. I agreed with her. I realized we all needed to stay on top of reminding them and calling them often, making sure they were following the restrictions we had kind of put in place for them. Tables are turned, all our lives we took instructions, guidelines, guidance and rules from them as we were young children. But now the children are taking charge and giving the instructions and guidelines for them to follow. They were getting calls and reminders of safety and precautions instructions to avoid and prevent the virus from Choice, Paul, Godwin, Daisy, myself and yes their grandkids and other cousins and family members. Paul Jr, Geoff, Tapfuma, Ruvheneko, Anesu, Tapiwa to name a few of some of the calls and messages on the family chat group to emphasize their safety and precautions. We all love our Midhu and CK.

Madelien works full time as a Registered Nurse at one of the major hospitals here in Atlanta. She is a front line worker and usually works on a Post Med Surgical Unit. In the rise of the Covid-19 pandemic when cases were rising at a fast pace in late February. Their unit was turned into a covid-19 floor to cater for the rising need for caring for these patients. Elective surgeries were all postponed in order to meet the demand for the covid-19 patients influx. At the same time throughout the month of March she was super careful to wear her PPE (Personal Protective Equipment) and would strip her uniform in the garage as soon as she got home from work, and put her scrubs in a bag and leave her work bag in the trunk of her car. She would wear a gown and come into the house and go straight to the shower. 1st week of April she started having high fever, coughing and back pain.

These are symptoms we had been seeing on the news and she knew some of her patients who had tested positive of the virus at her job would have complained of similar symptoms. When she started having the symptoms she informed her job and decided to quarantine herself from the kids and me. She went to get a Covid 19 test, her results came back negative. This did not make sense to us because her symptoms were not getting any better. This we both believed was a case of a false negative test. They were reporting at the time the inaccuracy of some tests was giving up to 33% false negative results. That is a high percentage of inaccuracy.

We however decided to maintain the quarantine precautions for the next 2 weeks. She moved to the guest bedroom. She had mild symptoms but we wanted to maintain precautions regardless. Kurai and Kayla were not allowed to go into her room to see her for any reason, we had to explain to them about the importance of mom not having any contact with them until she felt better. They were quick to understand because talk about corona was everywhere including all social media platforms and the television and obviously on their electronic gadget feeds.

I took over preparing meals and all chores in the house, with some help from Kayla and Kurai a times. I would prepare breakfast, lunch and dinner for Madelien and take her food to the door in her room. We dedicated one bathroom just for her and put a big note on the door, "Mom's Bathroom, Do Not Use".

We maintained these precautions for the two weeks she was in isolation. The cooking from yours truly, kept rolling heads, I believe because the food tasted so good.

Now I have improved my cooking skills so much that I am thinking of starting a food kitchen or restaurant. Kurai and Kayla feel I should not consider that option. Unfortunately Madelien had lost her sense of taste so she really could not judge or suggest otherwise in my favor. We however managed to make it work. Ordering out was not an option because we could not go out to eat as a family, and it would become very costly. Occasionally I would order out but the majority of meals I brought my A game chef skills.

I am going back to my whatsapp group messages, after announcing to a close group of friends that I had contracted the virus. Victoria, one of the members asked a legitimate question. Where do you get it from, Baltimore or Georgia? I in turn backtracked about 2 weeks prior to figure out and trace my contacts (contact tracing). My exact response in that group chat was...

"I was here in Atlanta on Thursday the 16th and Friday the 17th. Went and met with Bernard at the construction site both days for like one hour each day, discussed some work, ideas and changes with the project manager. I also met with my Atlanta tax office manager and partner Tiffany to discuss operations while I would be out of town. I went back to work from home after the meetings both days. Friday night I travelled to Baltimore by road because I did not want to risk flying and catching the virus at the airport or from other passengers on the plane.

I did not have contact with any other individuals until I met with three of my staff (Fatima, Mia and Rhodesia) briefly on Saturday afternoon and the four appointments I had scheduled that Saturday afternoon. By then there was a mandatory order by the Maryland governor for everyone to wear a mask. Everyone I met in Baltimore wore a mask including myself. Sunday I woke up with a fever and headache. I was feeling warm and had some back joint pain. I checked my temperature, it was 101.8F I knew this was abnormal.

As the day progressed, I felt weaker and my temp was not subsiding, my headache was not going away. Madelien and I decided after we discussed my symptoms and how I was feeling, that she fly to Baltimore on Monday afternoon and we drive back to Atlanta together. I was not in a condition to drive back to Atlanta alone. I cancelled all business appointments and meetings I had made for the week due to the medical emergency. We drove back to Atlanta on Tuesday morning." I asked Victoria in the group to grade my summary, and she gave me an A for the detailed contact tracing.

I know I gave that narrative of my possible contraction of the virus. I felt so confident we took all the precautions at home for me to have any chance of having gotten the virus, but then this is a virus that nobody at this time can say with certainty they knew much of. The incubation period and when it is most contagious and from the time Madelien started showing symptoms which eventually went away. The medical specialists and experts on the spread of the pandemic statedat the time a 2 to 14 day incubation period. All we can do and could do was speculate and second guess. To try and trace all my contacts the previous 2 weeks. Which can be difficult to do. All contacts between work, the construction project, the tax offices, stores, gas stations. It could possibly be from anywhere and difficult to pinpoint. This is why recommendations now and in hind site should have been made more strict for hand washing, social distancing, mask wearing and avoiding crowds and unnecessary gatherings, avoiding shaking hands and hugging. By this time, travel was limited to essential travel only, but one would still have a possible large number of contacts even with the restrictions in place.

The Monday morning before Madelien flew in, I toughened myself to go into the office. I was sweating on and off, having intervals of chills and sweats, my head was also pounding. Fatima, my personal assistant and office manager for several years was already at the office in Baltimore, but she had to leave as soon as I got to the office for a dental appointment. As soon as I got in the office, she sensed and noticed I was not my usual self and asked if I was ok, or needed anything before she left for her appointment. I told her not to worry, I was doing fine and she should go ahead and leave for her appointment. I sat on my desk and decided to send a group message to my siblings that I was not feeling well, I described my symptoms to them on the group chat. We communicate often in group texts and constantly communicate via whatsapp. In this Corona virus epidemic era I wanted to share with them what was going on with me at that time, I definitely did not feel normal. I felt extreme fatigue as I sat in the chair, with no energy to even turn my computer on. I felt so tired like I had just run a marathon. I managed to send the message to my siblings as I just sat at my desk staring at the black computer screen I had no strength to turn on.

My sister Choice called me immediately in alarm from Zimbabwe, and I struggled to express much to her, my voice was weak, and I was struggling to talk. We spoke briefly due to my weariness. Two minutes after that call, Paul called and asked of the same questions and concluded I needed medical attention, stating I needed to go to the Hospital immediately. The truth is I was not comfortable with the idea of going to hospital. With the stats I was seeing on the news daily. I felt that was the last place I wanted to go. I felt I was better in a home environment and could treat myself from home and recover, I remember my voice sounding extremely weak and lethargic during the conversation. After the brief call my phone kept ringing back to back from numbers I was not familiar with. I eventually picked up. I really was not in the mood to be talking and answering the same questions or explaining anything at the time. The pain was real, the thumping headache and back ache. "Hi this is Jade, Shami's cousin, we need to make a plan so you go to the ER as soon as possible for evaluation, what is your address we set that up and call 911. I reluctantly agreed. Paul's wife Shami, has a cousin Jade who also lives in Maryland Washington area and was advised of my condition and given my phone number to arrange for my hospital transfer. She works in radiology and has medical background, I later found out. She would call a few more times until everything got setup and situated. Everything happened so fast within that 30 minute period, 911 was called and I was transported for evaluation at an area hospital close to my office. My vitals were checked, and I got some pain medicine and muscle relaxant. I was having muscle pain and at this time my head was still throbbing, and I still felt pain in my lower back.

I got stabilized with some pain medicine. By this time my temperature had subsided, I was asked if I had a sore throat and I told them no, they also asked if I was having difficulty breathing, but I was not having any of those symptoms. In hind sight the questions they were asking were to determine if I was a candidate to be tested for the covid-19 virus, maybe due to my stabilized vitals and improved symptoms at the time, there was no need to get the covid-19 test at the time. After I got stabilized, I just rested and slept with no further symptoms or pain. My wife eventually arrived later that evening, and I was released from the hospital. We took an uber to go back to my office to get my vehicle, and then went to get a good night rest so we embark on the road trip back to Atlanta the next morning.

I am so proud of Madelien. She took the flight to Baltimore Washington International on the news of my state, and drove back to Atlanta with me nonstop the following day. The only stops we made were for fuel and rest area stretches for a few minutes. Ten and a half hours later, we arrived to Atlanta. I told her. "I am proud of you, and thank you for doing this." She just looked at me with those big beautiful brown eyes with a smile and said, "You are welcome baby."

As soon as we got back home, we made a decision that I isolate. We laughed about switching roles. I did not want to have any contact with the kids too, just in case I had contracted the virus somehow.

Madelien opted to move back to the guest room where she had been isolating a few days prior. We made the master bedroom my new living arrangement and setup a little microwave on top of the little bedroom fridge which was already in there. We brought in an electric kettle, tea bags and coffee, water and Juice with a little fruit basket. I totally have no reason to leave the room, so I protect the family because we both suspected the symptoms I had experienced were Covid-19 related.

On Wednesday afternoon we went to a drive up Covid-19 testing center that is about a mile up the street from our home. I got the test done and was advised they would call me with the results in 48 hours. We went back home and I went back into isolation, avoiding the kids. I maintained to wear a mask. We also setup a video-tele appointment with my primary physician who I advised of my symptoms, he prescribed (Zpack) Azythromycin ABT, Hyrochloroquin, prophylaxis in anticipation that I was having the virus. I questioned the chloroquin prescription because I had started reading bad reviews about the drug and how the CDC was not recommending it to treat covid-19. Along with these drugs, my primary doctor also sent a script for Tramadol to combat the severe headaches that I was having constantly.

Taking Ibuprophen was not recommended because research and tests for covid patients showed taking drugs which are NSAID (non steroidal anti inflammatory drugs). These drugs do not interact well together and can cause flaring and further complications. So in addition to Tylenol to reduce the fever, the Tramadol 50mg was to combat the headache. We picked up these medications from the pharmacy as soon as we arrived in Atlanta.

All day Thursday I stayed in the room. I checked my temperature periodically during the whole day and it stayed elevated, I would have periodic sweats and chills. My temperature would stay elevated, ranging between 100 to 102.5 degrees Fahrenheit, I would also have a lingering headache all day.

I took 1000mg of Tylenol to reduce the fever every 4 to 6 hours. I avoided laying down as all the time as I had seen and read that staying active and avoiding laying on your back would help slow down any potential buildup and blockage of airway. Lying in prone position, on your stomach is recommended. I am not one who sleeps in prone position, I am either on either side or my back, so this was different and uncomfortable way for me to lay down but after all I was reading and hearing, I knew this would benefit me. It was now about 11pm on Thursday night, I had been sitting in the chair most of the day, and trying to avoid spending much time in bed in that prone position. I had started coughing up phlegm the past 24 hours. This productive cough would not happen on a regular. I would not say coughing was a major symptom I had, but the few times I did cough, it would be productive. I took a Tramadol, my Z pack ABT dose, Vitamin C, Zinc and multivitamin before I lay in my unusual and uncomfortable prone position. I decided not to take the Hydrochloroquin because of all the negative reviews it was reading about and hearing medical experts state how it affected the heart rate and was said to increase the chances of death on coronavirus patients instead of having a healing effect. I ceased on taking that particular drug.

As the day progressed, I was getting more comfortable to lay on my stomach. I went to sleep after checking my temperature which was 100.5 and a slight headache persisted. Friday morning of May the 24th I got up at 7:30am, sat on the side of the bed for like a minute then proceeded to walk to the bathroom.

I felt dizzy and staggered back to sit on the edge of the bed. Something was wrong, my breathing was not normal, I was finding it difficult to breath.

I was having shortness of breath. I reached out to the pulse ox that was on the nightstand. My oxygen saturation was 79% this is low. Normal range should be preferably between 92 and 100%. I knew right away, this is not normal. I grabbed the thermometer and checked my temperature. It was 103.5 degrees. I reached for my phone and called Madelien immediately.

She rushed into the bedroom with her mask as usual practice, she looked panicked after I told her I could not breath. I was really having difficulty breathing and was gasping for air more and more. At this time, she rechecked my vitals and nothing have improved. My oxygen saturation had actually dropped further to 73%. She said immediately, we need to call 911 and have you go to the hospital for evaluation. I told her I was going to lay back down on my stomach and should feel better. As we had that discussion, I continued to have a sudden shortness of breath and immediately realized I needed oxygen more than anything else at this time. I agreed for her to call 911 right at that moment.

I got up with her assistance to go brush my teeth, and soon after that I heard the ambulance sirens, it took about 4 minutes from the time she called and the paramedics were knocking at the front door. I was still in my pyjama pants and t-shirt. I said to her, let me jump into the shower, she said that is not a good idea because your oxygen is low and possibly your blood pressure will drop even lower if you go into the shower and the hot water dilates your bloods vessels.

I never had time to change into anything else. I usually make sure I am looking on point before I step out of the house, but this situation was different.

The only thing I am thinking now as I was sitting on the bedroom bench, was oxygen. "I need oxygen." I felt like I was drowning.

The paramedic came in wearing his PPE (Personal Protective Equipment) as they had been told of my symptoms and as precaution were treating me like a positive covid-19 patient. He asked me a few questions and checked my vitals and to his surprise, my oxygen level was that low, reading 73% and I was still responsive and was able to walk out of my bedroom, down the stairs and out the main door to the ambulance where I sat in the stretcher and they put me into the ambulance. I did not get a chance to wake the kids up or hug them goodbye, I did not even get a chance to give Madelien a kiss or peck goodbye as our normal routine either one of us leaves the house or returns. We however exchanged a few words, I do not remember the conversation. I remember saying to her, call mom and dad and let them know. She said, "Ok baby, talk to you soon." As she handed me my phone and charger.

The ambulance door closed, we sat there idling for a couple of minutes. They hooked me up to an oxygen mask and set it at 15 liters. This brought life into me and I felt so relieved and brand new that I was breathing with no distress or difficulty again. I felt like hugging the paramedic. Never in my life do I remember relying on an oxygen tank to breathe. We take that for granted. At this moment in my head I was like. "Thank you Jesus. That you made these paramedics come to me with oxygen." Thank you for oxygen.

CHAPTER FIVE

Walk By Faith Not By Sight...

Mark 11:24 ESV. Therefore I tell you, whatever you ask for in prayer, believe that you have received it, and it will be yours.

WE HAVE A saying in my Zimbabwean language (Shona) that goes, "Chikuru kufema". Meaning, "The biggest thing is to breathe". Now this saying will forever make so much sense and have a deeper meaning to me.

I realize how in the spare of time my breathing was compromised and if I did not receive the 15 liters of oxygen when I did. I do not know if I had made it another 10 minutes alive. I can only wonder and speculate at this time.

I had really felt like I was being choked and drowning, finding it so difficult to breathe, until that oxygen was hooked to me. In the medical field, in any emergency or heirachy of importance in any situation. The most important aspect is airway, the breathing and heart rate. Important aspect of life, CPR and initial stability of any individual in distress.

When we arrived at the hospital, they unhooked my oxygen periodically from the vehicle to hook me to the hospital portable oxygen tank, the 30 seconds or less it took for that transition felt like a lifetime. I panicked, it felt like the paramedic was taking my life away and stopping my only lifeline, I wanted to shout out and ask him to plug the oxygen back on, but all I could do was look at him in a respiratory distress state, as I felt suffocated when he was switching the ambulance oxygen tank to the hospital portable tank. I felt as if I was drowning and being choked again. I gasped for air in desperate attempt to have him realze I needed to stay hooked on. This transition from the ambulance felt like a lifetime. Soon they hooked me to the hospital portable tank and pushed me into the hospital as I lay on the stretcher. I felt life come back to me again, I felt so relieved and grateful that I could breathe once the tubing was hooked back on. Thank you for reconnecting me to the oxygen tank I said to myself. My panic and distress disappeared, and I felt comfortable and thankful that I was now in a facility where they should have unlimited oxygen supply and experts who can help me with my condition. I am thinking several thoughts in my head. Moving on will I always rely on this artificial oxygen therapy? "If I do not have it constantly being administered to me, am I going to make it?"

This was a constant question I was debating in my head and was afraid someone might mistakenly turn the machine off and that will be the end of me. "Am I going to be put on a ventilator? Am I going to need artificial oxygen forever? Am I going to make it? Am I going to see my wife and children again? I did not see my kids before I left the house. The paramedics had called ahead and informed them of my symptoms and condition. They unerstandably had covid-19 precautions protocol as they checked me in.

They performed several tests on me upon my arrival, it seemed like every minute there was a procedure being done to me, blood draws, vitals, portable chest xray, EKG, covid-19 nasal test/swab, more blood work, I felt the great medical attention I was receiving was a blessing, and I am thankful for that moment because it somehow made me realize I was in a safe and competent environment. All this activity happened in the first thirty minutes of my arrival.

Another thirty minutes later, one of the doctors came in and introduced himself and advised me, I was Covid-19 positive and was going to be transferred to the covid unit for further treatment and isolation precautions. The doctor kept speaking but I was not listening to anything else after that point. I think he reassured me that they will do their best to treat me. He may have asked if I had any questions. I could not ask anything. I'm just numb at this point. I am sure my eyes had scared written all over them. I said to him. "Yes, I understand." I did not understand anything, I did not know anything.

The visuals and thoughts in my head is the increasing numbers of cases and deaths the country was experiencing. Also the fact that I am a black man, I felt the odds were not in my favor because the stats did not work out well for African Americans.

I am going to die. "God help me." Is a prayer I said to myself. The doctor advised me my chest xrays and EKG did show that my chest, lungs were very congested and possible signs of pneumonia, and hence the reason my airway is blocked, not clear and why I was having difficulty breathing. I had so many questions in my head but I could hardly comprehend everything the doctor was saying, it felt like a death sentence. Again he asked if I had any questions. I just stared at him in disbelief, maybe confusion and fear. "No sir, thank you." I said to him. He calmly encouraged me and wished me a speedy recovery and all the best as he left the room. What is going to happen to me? Will I get better and get out of this hospital? Healed? I started thinking of the news and headlines, the narrowing probability of survival when one is admitted into hospital, goes into ICU, or gets put on a ventilator. "I am dead!" Like I am being taken away into an isolation room on a Covid-19 unit. "God. Is this my last chapter, am I here to die? Will I ever see my family again?" I am thinking all this to myself. The final statement the doctor made to me was knowledge of my verbal consent. "If you get into cardiac arrest or stop breathing. Do you want the medical staff to resuscitate you and do everything they can to keep you alive or you want them to let you go comfortably? This question was so sobering. It made me realize the seriousness of my condition and death was a very possible option.

I stared straight into the doctor's eyes and gave the affirmative nod. "Yes, please resuscitate me." Was my response. Full measure to make me a full code and keep me alive. I am not ready to die I thought to myself. Soon the transfer team arrived, two individuals wearing gowns, gloves, facemasks, eye protectors, face shield and head gear covering every inch of their bodies as far as my eyes could see. They introduce themselves and told me they were there to take me up to the 19th floor secure Covid-19 unit. I say another prayer to myself. "No weapon formed against me shall prosper. "Lord I am going to come out of this. Thank you for healing me." I have heard preachers say and read several times. Words are powerful, and we speak it into existence. I was thanking God for healing as I declared victory and spoke it into existence.

"I will be healed, I will come out of this, thank you Jesus for healing me." I am saying all these short prayers in my head as I am being transferred to this dreaded unit where I will be in contact isolation and not be allowed to have any visitors or access to any family, friends or the outside world.

I am scared, I do not know what to expect, but I continue saying, "Thank you God for life, I will see my family again. I will breathe on my own again. I will be healed. Thank you Jesus". In the midst of my fear I kept praying and believing God will make a way somehow.

We arrived on the secure covid-19 unit on the 19th floor and I was transferred to my room. They helped me to transfer into the bed, and right behind them was a nurse who immediately came in and hooked me up to oxygen system in the room and set me up. A setup that was all ready and prepped for arrival of any patient I presumed.

The transition from disconnecting me from the portable oxygen tank to the room oxygen happened to fast I was happy they kept my oxygen flowing because at this time I knew as much as they did. My life and survival depended on it. Who would have thought. All my life I have never thought of the importance or direct impact oxygen has on an individual. We take it for granted. At least I know I did. I have breathed naturally all my life with no need for a non-rebreather mask or nasal cannula. I could not be without the artificial oxygen at this time, it was vital for my survival. Chikuru kufema.

The nurse introduced herself and oriented me to the room. She gave me the kitchen menu which had decent selection of meals and desserts. For the whole stay, all I had to do was call the kitchen and place an order for what I would want to eat for all meals. It was a very convenient setup. The room was a neat, cozy and private. I believe to make one feel as comfortable and as close to a homely setup as possible. I had a bathroom which had a shower and tub, a large mirror and shelves next to my bed, and behind the bed on the walls a lot of machinery, equipment and an oxygen outlet, monitors and screen. The bed was electric which I could control to be in any position that would make me comfortable by elevating the feet, or head to be in a sitting position or lying flat.

The same bed control had controls to remotely turn the television on and off and change the channels. I was also able to use the same remote by pressing the nurse call button and it would connect to the nurse station and I would be able to speak with the nurse or operator and let them know my request and concern and get attended to if need be or any back and forth communication. To the right of the room was a comfortable recliner chair and an adjustable bed side table. The room was a pretty nice size room with a large wall to wall window which gave a partial view of Atlanta on this 19th floor covid-19 unit which would be my isolation room for what I did not know at that time how long I would be in isolation for. I will say, it was a nice private room, the only difference from a competitive at minimum a 4 star hotel room was that it had medical equipment, monitors, tubing and oxygen and blood pressure and oxygen monitoring ports on the room wall. Though I felt isolated, it was a nice comfortable cozy room. I lay in bed with my head slightly elevated and getting familiar with my surroundings as the nurse stated she was going to insert an intravenous line in my arm and start antibiotic therapy which was ordered to help treat my condition. All this is happening while I am receiving oxygen continuously at a high rate, it had been reduced to 10 liters. The nurse went to collect all the supplies and came back to start and setup the IV which I at this time did not have a clue would run continuously with different antibiotic treatments for the next seven days. After I had gotten some medicine to calm me down and relax me, my heart rate which had been racing and running high, was much better. The normal average adult range of heart rate or beats per minute it between 60 and 100, my heart rate was 122. Soon after I got settled and all hooked up to these IV lines, heart monitor and constant oxygen therapy being administered. Oxygen is surely vital for life and God gives it to us as he gives life to all living organisms.

Oxygen truly is vital for survival, there are no options for that fact. The kitchen phoned on the room phone and asked me to give them an order from my menu, what I would like for lunch and for dinner, and if I needed any snacks or dessert.

About an hour later, the tech came in the room with me meal and asked me if I needed anything else before she walked out, she would make sure I had my ice water. Whoever would enter my room would be all dressed with personal protective equipment, gown, mask, gloves, eyewear, face shield and some head covers. The nurse and tech would try to group everything they needed to do in my room to avoid frequency and continued contact with me. However everyone in the hospital really made me feel welcome and were respectful, caring and friendly.

That same afternoon, the doctor came in and introduced herself and briefly told me about my plan of care. I asked her based on what she is used to seeing, with my condition, what was my prognosis. How long was I going to be in isolation, would my condition improve? She was honest and direct with me and advised me that the amount of oxygen I was requiring at the time was very high and based on the chest xrays and CT scans. They did see pneumonia in my lungs, my heart rate was too high and was not coming down, and my temperature remained high. Based on these facts she said to me. Anything is possible, I have seen people in your condition stay 10 days, some 2 weeks, some have stayed as long as 3 weeks or longer. Some have not made it unfortunately.

But we will do our best to treat you so you get better. 'I do not want to give you a timeline or idea that you will be discharged or may not require an intubation because I do not know at this time."

This was honest but not the news I wanted to hear. I was hoping to hear a more positive and guaranteed outlook and that I will be back home in a couple of days. She would be one of the same doctors who worked with me and plan of care until I got discharged.

As the doctor left the room, and I lay in the bed thinking. That was not the best of news. Some did not make it was definitely a reality. She did not have to emphasize that, I thought to myself. Though this was a fact, every day on the news I was seeing how people were dying. I had to be calm and not think of the negative. Maybe this was one of the reasons my heart rate (pulse) was running high. Fear of dying and anxiety. I had to change my mindset and not fear. **Philippians 4:6–7 NKJV. Be anxious for nothing, but in everything by prayer and supplication, with thanksgiving, let your requests be made known to God, and the peace of God, which surpasses all understanding, will guard your hearts and minds through Christ Jesus.**

The next couple of days did not go very well, my condition did not improve. I would have my heart monitor connected at all times so the nurses and staff at the nurses station will be able to see if my heart rate dropped or drastically increased at a dangerous rate. A couple of times I would get a call on my bed remote from the nurse or whoever was monitoring my machine that they could not see any activity. I would respond and tell them I am not in any distress. The nurse would come into my room and reconnect all by ports to make sure they were all in position and sending signal to the monitor. Apparently during my movement from side to side or as I attempted to sleep on my stomach I may have dislodged one of the ports connected to my chest, which would sent a signal that there was no activity, which would make the nurse call to check if I was ok.

It was about 3:40am on Monday morning, I remember opening my eyes and looking at both sides of my bed were nurses and a doctor including techs I had not seen prior. The monitor showed no activity on the board, the nurse called to check if all was well with me.

I did not respond this time, per hospital policy she came in to check on me. Apparently I had stopped breathing, this time all my ports were connected properly to my chest. The reason I did not respond to the call was, I was unresponsive. In hind sight, I am so thankful for the monitors and fast acting nurse who came to check on my non response to make sure the reason no heart signal was being sent to the monitor was because I had dislodged the ports. This was clearly not the case this time, I had really stopped breathing and my heart had stopped.

I found out after the fact. The nurse called for the hospital protocol to perform CPR on me to bring me back to life, I do not recall any of it obviously because I had blacked out and cannot remember anything.

I probably stopped breathing in my sleep and prompted the emergency medical intervention for pulmonary resuscitation. All I remember is when I opened my eyes, I had at least five individuals in my room and one of the nurses was doing compressions on my chest and everyone else looked very focused and attentive with eyes on me. My bed was flattened to make the chest compressions more effective. I am grateful because I was told my nurse that night after everything had settled and I had come back around, that I had not responded to the call when my monitor was not showing activity, when the nurse came in to check on why I was not answering or responding to the call. The nurse found me unresponsive with no pulse and had to call for an emergency code to perform CPR on me to revive me. **Psalm 51:14–19 GNT—Spare my life, O God, and save me, and I will gladly proclaim your righteousness...**

Isaiah 41:10—So do not fear, for I am with you. Do not be dismayed, for I am your God. I will strengthen you and help you. I will uphold you with my righteous right hand.

Psalm 32:4 ESV—Even though I walk through the valley of the shadow of death, I will fear no evil, for you are with me. Your rod and your staff, they comfort me.

Ecclesiastes 7:17 ESV—Be not overly wicked, neither be a fool. Why should you die before your time.

Ephesians 2:8–9 For by grace you have been saved through faith. And this is not your own doing, it is the gift of God, not a result of works, so that no one may boast. I would remain in isolation in my hospital room with no access to any physical outside world, except the nurses, doctors and technicians who were super geared and protected not to have any contact and maintain the isolation. The few times I had to be transferred to the x-ray and CT Scan, and ekg departments there on the Covid unit, I kept seeing and hearing commotion, some patients getting CPR and being coded, overhead pages of emergencies in room xxxx. Clearly some people did not make it. I saw lifeless bodies and body bags being taken off the floor. This would be a sight the few times I had to be taken out of my isolation room to go to Ct scan and xrays departments. I would just say a prayer for their souls.

On the tombstone of my little sister is the verse, **Isaiah 57:1–2 The righteous perish and no one takes it to heart, the devout are taken away, and no one understands that the righteous are taken away to be spared from evil. Those who walk uprightly enter into peace, they find rest as they lie in death.**

These last 8 words of verse 2 have given me comfort with my sister, as I believe and love the fact that she will never feel pain or suffering on this earth again, as she sleeps in the Lord.

That is the same comfort and peace I believe all those who did not make it will not suffer again, they will never have pain or gasp and yearn for oxygen and struggle to breathe again. They are resting as they lie in death. I could only imagine as I sat back in my isolation room, how much of this is happening all day everyday as some succumb to this virus and do not make it. Truly sad and scary to think. Their loved ones and families may have called 911 just like what happened to me just under a week prior, and not have a chance to hug their loved ones or tell them they love them. Can you imagine if the last conversation with their loved one was a fight or an argument or of anger, then never got a chance to amend, or to say sorry, or make peace.

Suddenly life happens and corona can hit you hard. You go out on emergency 911 ambulance call, they arrive and take you in within 4 minutes from the time you call. Which they did in my case, then you get taken away. Some may never have a chance to go back home to say I love you, I am sorry, or to hug their children or spouse. When you are on that edge and you cannot breathe and gasping for air, you may ask God to give you one last chance to make amends or to say something to someone or make amends for what you may have held in you forever.

It may be a grudge or anger. Sometimes you ask God, please give me a chance to say to whoever it may be… I love you. Forgive me. I am sorry. Or, yes I forgive you.

On Wednesday evening, two days after my scare. I had a sobering discussion with my doctor who in his final rounds for the day came into my room and advised me of my CT scan results,

current progress and plan of care. Basically, she advised me that based on the scan results, my pneumonia had grossly spread and infiltrated to my right lung, and as much as I was getting IV antibiotics to treat the pneumonia, it looked as if it had spread and seemed ubiquitous according to the latest readings.

This may had been a reason why my breathing was not improving. The doctor did a weaning test to see if I could handle having the oxygen removed and if my body can tolerate the lack of artificial oxygen being administered, before she removed the oxygen, my saturation percentage was 98% while on 10 liters of oxygen administration, after removing and turning off the oxygen, I started feeling dizzy and like someone was choking me, stopping my oxygen intake, I was gasping for air again. It was so uncomfortable and my saturation dropped drastically and quick to 84%, clearly this meant that I was not ready to be weaned off of the oxygen. I could not make it past one minute, I was quickly asking the doctor to turn the oxygen back on. She turned the oxygen back on and my saturation shot back up to 95-96-97 and stabilized at 98% again. This was a big relief and everything felt normal. No more respiratory distress or panicking. I was already taking blood thinners prophylaxis to prevent blood clots.

The doctor asked me if I was making use of the incentive spirometer because it was critical to help strengthen my lungs and give them some exercise because I was not being active and mostly bed ridden. I was advised that at the current rate, the next morning they planned to escalate me to the ICU unit and put me on a ventilator because my breathing was not improving and it was an option that would be the best resort based on my condition and lack of improving. I listened to this news in disbelief, as it seemed like things were getting worse for me, I was on a downward spiral. It felt like I was going through my last chapter and going to my final phase of life on this earth. Hearing the doctor tell me I was going to be put on a ventilator the next morning was the worst news I had heard since I was admitted. I am thinking, once I am on a ventilator, that is the last phase and there is no other treatment beyond that, once I am relying on this machine to breathe for me, It will be hard for me to recover and breathe on my own, reason why the death rate of people who end up on a ventilator is high. I was scared and worried. I started praying with my eyes shut as I listened to Pandora on the Praise and Worship genre. I was telling God, I believe in him, I will not have premature death. **Psalm 102:24—Do not take me away, my God, in the midst of my days, your years go on through all generations.** That Wednesday night I remember calling my father and asked him to send me a voice note of one of my favorite hymms. Both my parents are still very active in the church and one of their calling is singing in the church choir. They have been choir members for as long as my memory can go and I enjoy listening to their beautiful voices. Their church has won several gospel choir prizes over the years. My request that I really wanted to listen to from my father was a shona song, "Handikukanganwe Mwana Wangu" (I will never leave you of forsake you my child). I am glad he obliged to do the song and to put icing and a cherry on top, it was a voice note of both him and mom. I have that voice note saved in my phone today, and is one of the most heartfelt and warm message I have received, it came with a prelude of get well wishes and encouragement. I simply loved it. Thank you again Mdilo and Midhu.

CHAPTER SIX

Faith Over Fear... Mental Toughness

Psalm 118:17 ESV—I shall not die, but I shall live, and recount the deeds of the Lord.

TWO HOURS LATER after I got this message from the doctor, I believe it soon after shift change. The nurses worked 12 hour shifts from 7:00am to 7:00pm. It was about 7:30pm, the oncoming shift nurse came into my room. It is unfortunate I do not recall her name because she was God sent, my angel. This nurse changed my perception and my feeling of fear and despair into belief, faith and victory. As she came in to introduce herself for the twelve hour shift she had just started and to administer my new IV bag and to check my vitals, she said to me. "Mr Masuta, do you have children?" In my soft lethargic voice I said, "Yes". "How many", she asked soon after. "I was looking at your chart and just got report on your condition and plan of care, you may be escalated to the ventilator and critical ICU. I need you to at some point get some strength to get up out of bed, go to the large mirror across up from your bed, no. Infact, I take that back. I need you to walk to the window, look outside the window and say to the world as you look out that window. I am coming back. Believe this as you tell the world. You will go back home to your children and you will not give up. A lot of people hear bad news and fold, they give up. You will not accept defeat, you will fight back and against fear or death. I want you to tell yourself you will be healed. The mind is a powerful thing." I will never forget this lady, I believe she was God sent. What she told me in that moment gave me a new outlook, revived my faith and made me see the light at the end of the tunnel. Instead of feeling down and out as if I was being ushered to death, I suddenly felt a burst of new energy in spirit. It did not instantly transfer physically, but she made me feel confident, and made me change my mindset and started believing from that moment, I will heal, I will survive. The total opposite feeling compared to 2 hours prior when the doctor had given me the possible ventilator news. It was probably close to midnight. I gathered myself to walk to the large window. I did exactly as she told me to do. **Hebrews 11:1—Now faith is the assurance of things hoped for, the conviction of things not seen.**

Psalm 46:10—Be still, and know that I am God

I pulled open the blinds and looked out to the city of Atlanta, the high rise buildings and bright shining city lights. I stood at the window in my room on the 19th floor, staring out into the world. I almost said verbatim how the nurse had expressed it to me. I was thanking God for healing and believing every word I spoke as I looked out that window. "I will heal, I will get better, I will see my children again, I will see Madelien again, I will get my health back and live to tell of the glory of God." I was standing there being thankful for the gift of life and how God has been good to me. I stood staring out the window, having a one on one conversation with God it felt like. Maybe 30 minutes passed as I just stood there, thinking of my life, my path, what I was thankful for and just reflecting. Above all, the main take away is I was declaring victory in that moment. I walked back to bed a few feet away and making sure I did not get my IV or oxygen tubing kinked or tangled up. My spirits were high and I felt a positive shift in energy as I laid back down in prone position making sure I did not dislodge my heart monitor and that my oxygen pipe was flowing with no interruption.

Luke 1:37—For nothing will be impossible with God.

I slept in no distress for the rest of the night. Thursday morning was my miracle morning and turning point. I got woken up by the nurse to check my vital signs at 6:00am, my vitals were not all within normal limits, my respirations were 26, this is considered rapid breathing, my oxygen saturation was 91%, again, this is on the low end. The oxygen I was receiving through the tubing was still connected to me running at 5 liters via the nasal cannula. As one nurse a few days prior to this morning had told me, "Breathe in through your nose like you are smelling a flower, breathe out like you are blowing out a candle." This will calm you down and bring your oxygen level back up. I did this breathing technique before she rechecked my oxygen saturation again. After about a minute and four good attempts of breathing in like I was smelling in a flower and blew out like I was blowing out a candle. Indeed, my oxygen saturation went up to 95% I did not go back to sleep after she left. I went back to lay in the prone position and started praying. Soon after I felt like my breathing was becoming compromised again. I did not call the nurse on the call light which was in my hand because she had just left my room fifteen minutes prior, I talked myself out of calling her back in the room. I decided at that moment, this is not going to be the normal life for me. I shall heal, I shall fight this. I had deep faith at that moment that I was about to be healed and get discharged soon. I was mentally tired and drained, but I told myself, fear is not an option. I am going to be healed. This is the conversation, prayer and pleading I made with God. As I was gasping for air (oxygen) not knowing if I was going to make it or not. As I lay in that hospital bed, plugged onto nasal cannula, receiving continuous oxygen and Intravenous medication still running in my veins. I plead with God to save me and I will in turn tell the world of his healing powers and how powerful and amazing he is. My bargain with God, "Lord save me, I will glorify your name." I spoke out loudly at least three times in my low energy voice as I squirmed in bed believing he would. **Jeremiah 17:14 ESV. Heal me, O LORD, and I shall be healed, save me, and I shall be saved, for you are my praise.**

Hebrews 11:1 ESV- Now faith is the assurance of things hoped for, the conviction of things not seen. At this point I was feeling an energy in me that I have not felt many times in my life. I had this conviction, this belief and trust that the energy was shifting, I continued to pray as I lay in bed, and kept believing. "God, I shall be healed, I am tired of being sick. I am not going to die. Thank you for healing me God, thank you for healing me." **Job 22:28 KJV—Thou shall also decree a thing, and it shall be established unto thee: and the light shall shine upon thy ways."** I got up from my prone position and sat on the side of the bed. As I sat there, I made a final plea with God. "Lord, I am about to take these oxygen tubing and cannula hooked to my face, giving me oxygen. I was born and lived all my life with no artificial oxygen, I am not going to rely on this any longer. I will breathe on my own." I took the tubing out of my nose and nostrils and threw it on the side of the bed. Deep down knowing I had not been able to function normally without the oxygen from the moment I was picked up from my home almost a week prior. **Philippians 4:6–7 ESV—Do not be anxious about anything, but in everything by prayer and supplication with thanksgiving let your request be made known to God, which surpasses all understanding, will guard your hearts and your minds in Christ Jesus.** My faith at that moment gave me the confidence to know that I would not get into respiratory distress or make my oxygen levels drop so low that I would pass out and get into a medical emergency. I really did not give failure as an option. I did not see God letting me down. I remained sitting upright on the side of the bed, no artificial oxygen connected to me. One full minute passed by, two minutes, three minutes. I was seeing instant results and thanking God for healing in that moment. It felt like a miracle in the making. I was breathing on my own with no artificial tubing or oxygen.

I took deep breaths in as if I was smelling a flower and would blow out like I was blowing out a candle, I did this repeatedly. **James 2:14 ESV—What good is it, my brothers, if someone says he has faith, but**

does not have works? Can that faith save him? I felt like I was on my road to recovery and that God had taken me on my plea and bargain. Four minutes pass by. I was excited and thanking God at the same time. I was breathing on my own and not needing artificial oxygen to stay alive. "Thank you Jesus. Thank you Jesus." **Ephesians 2:8 ESV—For by grace you have been saved through faith. And this is not your own doing, it is the gift of God.**

Mental Toughness—Hebrews 11:1 NIV—Now faith is being sure of what we hope for and certain of what we do not see.

Twenty minutes passed, thirty minutes passed. I still was breathing on my own without feeling shortness of breath, no respiratory distress. No panicking, I was breathing normal. I was in total awe and thankful, tears started rolling down my eyes as I said words of thanks to God. "Thank you Jesus, thank father. Thank you for healing me." At this moment I knew I was not going to have complications with covid-19 anymore. I just beat the corona virus. I am healed. About 7:30am, the nurse returned in my room with my breakfast tray and almost through it in the air with panic as she saw me casually sitting on the side of the bed with the oxygen tubing off my face and on the bed, all disconnected. "Oh my God!" She screamed, "You are not wearing your oxygen mask, are you ok? Who took it off?" As she rushed to put the breakfast tray on the table and attempt to place the oxygen tubing back on me. I moved my face away and I calmly responded. "I do not need the oxygen anymore. I took it off." I was not going to put the oxygen back on I expressed to her, as she rushed to get the pulse oxygen machine to check my oxygen level. To the surprise of both of us, the oxygen reading was 96% on room air. How long have you not had the oxygen on? she asked, I advised her it had been over an hour at that point. A shocking and pleasant development it was indeed. Less than 24hours prior from being on the verge of discussions of being escalated to a ventilator use and being told I will be transferred to the ICU unit if I kept having the breathing difficulties and non clearing pneumonia. To not needing any kind of oxygen less than 12 hours later, this was my miracle and turning point. The changing of my mindset, believing in healing, having the faith and seeing the results.

The nurse rechecked my vitals to make sure all my other parameters and health was in good standing. My blood pressure, heart rate, respirations and temperature were all within normal limits. The nurse was in disbelief as to how this was possible. The day before I had failed the test of being weaned from receiving artificial oxygen, daily from the day I had been admitted, the medical team and respiratory therapists would work with me and see if I would be able to tolerate removal of the oxygen for any significant time. Unfortunately, I would fail this test dismally daily and it was clear that I was nowhere close to breathing with no artificial oxygen being administered to me. This baffled the nurse because the normal progression would be weaning gradually, tapering down the oxygen requirement, until the patient no longer requires it and the strength test and need be signed off by the respiratory therapist and the doctor. God weaned me and discontinued the order for artificial oxygen. The prayer and faith I had with him that morning gave me belief that discontinued the artificial oxygen order. I took that leap of faith and told the nurse exactly that. "God weaned me off the artificial oxygen and discontinued the oxygen order." Indeed he did, indeed he did. She replied.

Faith and the Power of Healing

The first thing I did as soon as the nurse left my room was call my mother and my wife. I do not remember the order, but those are the calls I made. Feeling joyous. I remember saying to them, I took the oxygen off. I am breathing on my own. My voice was still lethargic, but you could hear the excitement in it, that excitement transferred in the voice of my mother when she heard my voice and I told her I was off the oxygen.

"Thank you God, Thank you Jesus. Mwari munundigonera." (God you are good to me). I remember hearing her say. "God is faithful mommy." I said to her, I also spoke to my father on that call and they both sounded super delighted and excited to learn of my condition and that I was off the oxygen therapy and on the road to recovery. "Our prayers have been answered, God is faithful." My mother said repeatedly as I could hear her voice crack with tears of joy.

The rest of the day I stayed off the oxygen, I told myself I will never use artificial oxygen again. I am glad to say, as I write this. That statement and belief has been true. I have not needed a drop of artificial oxygen from that morning. I have continued to breathe freely on my own using God's atmospheric oxygen and no tubing. I am healed.

Over the next 24 hours, the doctors came in and spoke with me. On Friday morning the doctor mentioned the xray from the CT scan still showed pneumonia in both my Lungs but was clearing up. The (corona virus) covid-19 is a virus that doctors and most in the health community are unable to treat. There is still no known cure. However, the doctor was not the only person surprised and shocked about my sudden progress and turnaround. She mentioned to me, I amazingly progressed and improved in a way that was beyond the usual recovery or prognosis based on my condition.

73

24 hours prior and less than a week prior to that moment, my condition was not good and my prognosis for recovery was very poor. She stated she was not sure how my condition turned around so fast and was almost in disbelief how I looked a lot better and was breathing on my own with no distress at all. She was not sure if the intravenous therapy and different antibiotics did it, or which treatment method it was but was just happy and pleased to see that I had recovered and healed. I remember telling her, "It was God. God healed me." She smiled and said, "Indeed, it is a miracle. I can believe that." I do not know what the doctor's belief or religion is, or if she is of the Christian faith, but she did agree with me in that moment. She then advised me, they will monitor me for another day or two, do more tests and blood work to make sure all is clear before I get discharged possibly on Saturday. This was the best news I had heard in that week, from once feeling like the end was near, and thinking I may die, having a roller coaster of emotions, fear of not making it and to now have this moment of victory. I saw the light at the end of the tunnel. I definitely believed, I was healed and in my head, thanked God for victory. Thank you Jesus. I am healed. "Thank you Jesus, for giving me life, I will see my wife again, I will see my children again, I will see my family and friends again." That feeling of getting another chance, it could have gone either way, knowing that this was the day I was supposed to be escalated to a more critical unit and be put on a ventilator, and the feared statistic that survival rate is less than 50% once one is put on a ventilator. I was not going to be part of that statistic, regardless which side of the 50% I fell on. **John 11:40—Then Jesus said, "Did I not tell you that if you believe, you will see the glory of God?"**

I was just happy and grateful to God for another chance on this earth again. Thank you God for saving me again, I thought. After the doctor left the room, I remained sitting in the recliner, I reached for my phone and called Madelien immediately. She could hear the excitement in my voice as soon as she answered. Just by my, "Hi baby…" she knew I had some exciting news and I could feel sense the excitement in her tone as well.

"What is it baby?" She quickly responded back. I gave her the great news and the great possibility that I will be getting discharged on Saturday. "I am coming home." We shared a moment of excitement and thanksgiving. Believing and thanking God that he had answered our prayers and the prayers of family and friends. "God is good, God faithful." After we hung up, I placed another call to my mother "Mwari anondida." (God loves me). She repeated that statement as she praised and thanked God for healing and saving me. My mother in this moment said to me. "Ro, God has been good to you. You need to live right and praise him. He has shown you mercy over and over and over. I want you to be obedient and forever thankful. You have a story to tell. You have a testimony my son. Your story will change a soul or souls. I am not saying go into preaching or anything like that. I am saying you need to do something to acknowledge that God has been good to you. Share your story and I believe your testimony will save a soul or change lives. God is good." This gave me pause as I began to think, what can I do? How can I show or express this sentiment? Mom is right. I said to her in that moment without thinking about it. "Mommy, I will write a book. I will talk about the goodness of God and how he has been great to me. I will talk of his glory."

In that same conversation I mentioned to her the bargain I had made with God the day before when I took my oxygen supply tubing off. She agreed with me and said if it is a book you are going to write and show the glory and greatness of God, follow through with it.

Keep your end of your bargain. Whatever you do, I believe you need to acknowledge and thank him.

Less than five minutes after we hung up, Daisy video called me from Australia. She had the biggest smile on her face, What she said next made me almost choke, I do not remember ever laughing so hard. After our short greeting and knowing I was healed and on the road to recovery, getting discharged. She said to me in an instructive tone. More than a suggestion, "Ro, you are going to buy some suits, and you are going to be a pastor. You shall go around the world preaching the gospel and tell people how God has saved you several times…" I bust out laughing so hard as she attempted to repeat the same statement. We both started laughing so hard, I promise I could not stop laughing. We laughed until I think she realized I was getting short of breath and it was becoming dangerous to keep laughing like that. I do not remember if I just hung up or she did, but that is as much as that conversation went. I kept laughing for several minute after that and whenever I remembered the statement and how she said it in a stern calm authoritative voice as she pointed her finger at me saying I will be a preacher. It was a hilarious moment indeed. I still laugh about it and how she expressed it to this day.

The rest of the day Thursday I was on my phone, looking back at messages from friends and family on different platforms. Texts, whatsapp, messenger, voice mails. I responded to a fraction of the ones I could. I just could not respond to all. I did speak to all my siblings and shared my discharge news and joy. They all shared the great news and excitement with me.

Friday came and I was just ready to be back home, I spoke to my sons Kurai and Panashe, they were both ecstatic of the news of me getting discharged. They did not have to worry or wonder what would happen to their dad anymore. It was a great feeling to know I was going to connect with my boys again. For my little princess Kayla, I do not know how else to imagine my life without her, and with the bond we have. I do not even want to think or imagine me not being in her life. I was super excited that I was going back home to my babies. Saturday discharge from the hospital was not coming fast enough. As the day progressed I still had the intravenous antibiotic therapy running in my veins, the labs came and drew more blood for more tests, I do not know what for and did not really care at that point as long as nothing came back to reverse the decision of my discharge orders to be released from the hospital and go back home. They could draw all the blood they wanted as far as I was concerned. I would be going home in less than 24 hours.

I went to bed Friday night all packed and ready. Like a student excited and looking forward to the first day of school. Saturday morning I kept looking at the clock as I was advised that my discharge paperwork will be ready and I can be picked up at 11am or anytime after that. I called Madelien and asked her to be at the hospital at 11:00am. Surely at 11:05am, the nurse came into my room to wheel me out to the pickup zone with my discharge paperwork and instructions. We got out and I stood out of the wheelchair and walked a few feet to the car. Visibly about 15 pounds lighter from the time I got admitted. I still had my face mask on, so did Madelien. As I got in the car, we hugged for a long moment. "I was scared" She said. I knew what she meant, as we continued to hug.

"How are the kids" I asked. We had to turn from the almost sad and somber moment that could have been if this hospital stay did not go our way. "They are excited that you are coming home and cannot wait to see you." We drove off and went to pick up some food for branch to have at home. We called mom and dad with joy and excitement while we waited in the car for the food. "Guess who is out of hospital? Whaoooooooooooo!!!" It was joyous and happy conversation.

John 11:40—Then Jesus said, "Did I not tell you that if you believe, you will see the glory of God?"

CHAPTER SEVEN

The Power of Prayer

As I expressed in my introductory chapter, I come from a very religious and prayerful family. When word got to my family about me being infected with the virus. One of my cousins, Daniel Muganiwa who lives in Harare Zimbabwe is now an ordained pastor and is assigned at Church of Christ Group in Sunningdale, Mbare area as one of the pastors. He formed a whatsapp prayer group on my behalf. This group consisted of my parents, my siblings including myself and some family members. This group was geared up for prayer mode. I only got to learn and read about it and what transpired on the Thursday afternoon as I sat in the recliner in my isolation room. Symptom free, breathing on my own, feeling brand new. After I made calls to my family and spoke to my wife and kids, I listened to voice mail messages which were full at the time. I felt the love and care from listening to a lot of concerned family and friends, work mates, business partners, and church members. I went through my social media platforms and checked my text and whatsapp messages. The Friday, one day before discharge, my niece Ruvheneko sent me a well put video that had her parents, Geoffrey, Tapfuma, herself, and Reina. This video compilation was so warm and motivating. They each sent warm words of encouragement, wishing for my speedy recovery and hope. This video made me realize how special and important family is. I felt loved. A few family members also started calling and texting, Paul Jr and his wife video called me from South Africa, I also spoke to all my siblings and as they had heard of the happy discharge news. I started going through my texts, voicemail and social media messages and whatsapp, text messages from various friends and family.

This took me most of the afternoon as I was clearly touched and humbled that so many people cared and left such heartfelt and warm messages. Somehow word got out to so many people, and some individuals I had not spoken to or heard from in years and very long periods of time. Some were from people I kept in touch with on a regular, some were old friend from high school and from college. To name a few, Clint, Charles, Daniel, Kudzanai, Tonde, Marshall, Castawell, Noel, Ethel, Pam, Natasha. Another friend, Chiedza put me on a prayer request through members of her church and pastor from Texas. My primary physician Dr. Ojo also stated he forwarded my name in a prayer request at his church.

The most active message thread I read was from the family prayer group created by my cousin Daniel. The specific prayer group has 25 participants, as mentioned, my parents, siblings, some aunts, uncles and cousins. I use the present tense because after I healed and got discharged, we never dismantled the group but decided to keep it as a faith and healing group. Praying for one another and growing together in faith. We named it "God Is Faithful." Reading back in the group messages as I sat in the chair, I was overwhelmed to learn how the family was praying day in and day out. They set schedules and time tables and teams to pray and fast on alternating days. Praying for my healing and recovery. "All this for me?" I thought. Wow. Thank you family. I am glad it did not end with me and we continue to cover each other in prayer and share our trials, tribulations and will continue to pray and share testimonies of how great God is. Indeed he is a healing and powerful God.

1 John 5:14–15 NKJV: Now this is the confidence we have in him, that if we ask anything according to his will, he hears us. And if we know that he hears us, whatever we ask, we know that we have the petitions that we have asked of him. An army of praying warriors prayed on my behalf, locally and worldwide. My aunt, sister to my dad (auntie Esther) I learnt called my father the Monday after I had been in the hospital for four days and stated to him, "Brother, do not worry, I spent the day at the top of the mountain yesterday in prayer, speaking to God to heal Rumbayi. Do not worry, I had a long prayer and spoke with God. Baba wedu will be fine." Baba wedu (Our dad). I was named after my grandfather and she was comforting her brother stating "our father will be fine, he will heal. God will heal him. **John 11:40—Believe—Then Jesus said, "Did I not tell you that if you believe, you will see the glory of God?"** My mother's sister (auntie Vhena) also spoke with me on how she had gone in deep prayer mode, pleading with God to save me and heal me. I have an aunt and uncle in Texas (The Matopodzi family), along with their daughter Tendayi would call and send prayer messages and words of encouragement.

The church members where my parents attend in Harare also prayed for me consistently. Their pastor (Marange) called and prayed with me that Friday, pastor Chinyerere also helped pray with my parents and give them verses of encouragement. They both shared scriptures of healing and faith. It was amazing to learn that people I do not know or have never met were in my corner praying for my healing and recovery. **Matthew 18:19–20 ESV. Again I say to you, if two of you agree on earth about anything they ask, it will be done for them by my father in heaven. For where two or three are gathered in my name, there am I among them.** I have not been a consistent tither, however it is something I am working on and know I should do better.

However I do contribute to the church often and help individuals outside of the church, the ones in need and do my best to feed the hungry. I had forgotten about this gift to the church, but my father reminded me. In 2016, Madelien and I decided to send a significant amount of money to my parent's church in Zimbabwe to help them upgrade their church, they decided to do the entire church floor tiles with the money that we sent. Our gift covered the labor and materials to do the entire church. The pastor then was very thankful for the gift to the Lord's house and announced at the church that Mr and Mrs Masuta's son who lives in Atlanta USA was able to gift the church with the new tiles. Though the church has a different pastor, most of the members remain the same and once they heard of my sickness. My parents tell me that a lot of members went to task and asked God to save me because I had been there for the house of the Lord. They asked God to spare my life because I had been there for his house and donated to his cause. "Lord, we now are able to kneel in comfort praising you with the floor your child donated to us. Save him. Give him more life." Are the prayers my mom and dad say the church members were praying. I had forgotten about the donation we made to the church and the renovations at the time. Not to equate the prayers to monetary value, but the gesture and gift we made left a lasting mark to most of the church members who went to cry to God to save me and spare my life when they heard I was critically ill with covid-19 virus.

The list of family and friends who sent me messages is long. I felt encouraged, I felt loved. It was such a great motivator and I must say, gave me wings and the extra energy and an uplifting and thankful spirit. I felt with such an army all around the world, friends and family, people that did not even know me before this hospital stay. It was just encouraging and humbling.

I knew God will not disappoint this big army of prayers. I felt the spirit of God and the fact that I was going to get more life. I surely will always encourage and believe in praying in numbers and crying out to God in masses is a great thing that God honors.

Philippians 4:6–8 ESV: Do not be anxious about anything, but in everything by prayer and supplication with thanksgiving let your requests be made known to God, which surpasses all understanding, will guard your hearts and your minds in Christ Jesus. Finally, brothers, whatever is true, whatever is honorable. Whatever is just, whatever is pure, whatever is lovely, whatever is commendable, if there is any excellence, if there is anything worthy of praise, think about these things.

Thank you mother for your prayers. I know you pray for us every day, you tell me you pray for me all the time, you send me prayers by text or in voice notes, you cover us all in prayer. Whenever you visit us or when I come home to visit. Listening to your powerful and overarching prayers gives me goose bumps. As a little child or young boy, I would roll my eyes at times with Tendai or Daisy when you started going deep into your prayers, touching everyone by name from dad all the way to Tendai. Now I cherish those prayers and love to hear them when you pray, no prayer is too long for me anymore. I appreciate and thank you for covering us all in prayer, including all our spouses and your grandchildren.

CHAPTER EIGHT

Family and Personal Trials and Tribulations

DAISY IS THREE years my senior, her birthday is in February 14 (Valentine's day), an easy one to remember. Growing up, we have always been very close, she is who I played games with the most, the one I would confide secrets with and hung around the most. Because of the age difference with my older brothers, I would want to spend more time and do things with them as a little boy but I would not fit in. I was too young to go hang out with the boys, go to movies or parties and sports games, though I would hear them discuss about their weekends, dates and missions and would just hope one day I would be able to fit in the discussions and be part of the boys club. However, from the time I was in primary school all the way to after about my fourth year in high school Daisy was my next of kin, my go to person. Tendai, was four years my junior and I would find myself with a sense of big brother mentality and I was more of a corrective figure and felt she was the only one I could teach and lead, I was more of big brother mentality but at our early ages in primary school, I felt grown and would want to spend more time with the older siblings and did everything in my ability to make sure I fit in and wanted them to recognize me more. I never felt in competition with any of my siblings but as we grew, at times we would play different games just for the fun and enjoyment, not care much as who won. Laughing and enjoying each other. Weekends and school holidays were the best as cousins would visit and spend parts of the holidays at our house and we would play outside all day til the sun went down. Games like hide and seek, hop scotch, rounders, cricket, basketball, cards games, checkers, chess, soccer, dodge ball… think of all the games you can come up with, we probably played them all. School holidays would be more fun because the more would be merrier, cousins and friends such as Brighton, Blessing, Tonderai, Tendayi, Pfungwa, Munyaradzi, Taka, Godfrey, including some of Daisy and Tendai's friends, Tendai, Farai, Jane, Emily, Terrence, George to name a few. Norman, my childhood partner in crime and cousin. Him and I would do the most, our escapades would require another book on its own. I believe there was only one or 2 TV channels on Zimbabwe broadcast at the time. This was before the introduction of satellite TV and the internet, and mobile phones in the mid 90's. There were three radio stations, and ours would always be locked onto radio 3. This was the channel

that played urban and international music, the latest music in the soul, R
&B, and hip hop charts.

Daisy was the person I spent a lot of my childhood time and gravitated to, after school and on weekends. Other times I would hang out with
Terrence (our next door neighbor), we were in the same grade and class
from grade 1 to grade 7.

When I was in 5th grade, Daisy was in her last year of primary school.
She was made school head girl. Being chosen head girl or head boy is a
position usually chosen for academic achievements or athletic ability and
sometimes just for leadership skills and presentation. This was a prestigious position awarded to the most examplary student in their final year.
Every school in Zimbabwe has chosen students in their final year, a selected
number of students known as prefects, what may be known as school monitors, and among them. A deputy head and a head are chosen. She did our
family proud by being chosen to be a head girl, regardless of the fact that
our father was chairman of the Parents Teachers Association, a position he
maintained until Tendai graduated grade 7. Daisy was quite the athlete, she
played volleyball, tennis, swimming and netball, and had great leadership
skills, I credit my parents for the leadership trait and character in all of us.
Tendai and myself eventually became prefects as well at primary school.
After Daisy graduated from primary school, she went to boarding school
away from home. These are the years, Tendai and myself started spending
more time and connecting. When I was in grade 7, Tendai was in grade
4, I was now looking at advancing to high school and started focusing
and figuring out which high school I would attend. I did not want to be
in boarding school, because I wanted to be closer to home and being a
mamas boy I felt it would be difficult to go away from home. I ended up

getting accepted at a few high schools, I chose Prince Edward, where both my brothers attended. As I got into high school and started figuring and maneuvering my way, this transition was made smooth by the fact that I had an older brother protecting me. My first year in high school, was Godwin's last year. He was in upper 6. I had my protector.

I quickly got acquainted to the school and I did not get bullied as some of the students in form 1, once the other older students knew I was Sutas's young brother, I was untouched and had a very smooth first year. That transitioned me well into form 2 with great confidence. I kept the mentality and confidence through high school to when I decided to go into boarding the final 2 years. Playing basketball, rugby, becoming a prefect as well in those final two years at Prince Edward, which was regarded in high esteem. I was known as a what they termed as a legend in those final two years at Prince Edward Boys High School.

Through life, we all go through ups and downs. Most of us go through several of emotions and stages. Joy, happiness, sadness, grief, failure, excitement, setbacks, celebration, success… Daisy is no exception. I have asked her permission to include this portion of the book, I would have included Tendai too, but because she is no longer with us to give the consent, I will talk a little about Daisy. Tendai and Daisy, these two siblings are ones I grew ever so close with, shared a childhood and adolescent years, all the way to Tendai's passing. To date, I feel so comfortable and confident to talk about Daisy or Tendai, because they both let me into their lives and we have grown close over the years. This is my mother's prayer, for all her six children to be close and to not fight or have drifts, to be happy and care for each other. To love one another. Midhu says all the time, "I pray to God to make sure all my children get along, and it makes me so happy to know there is love shared between all my children and grandchildren." We have had our ups and down, and common fights as siblings, but I must say. We have made my mother proud. As we continue to build that perfect union, love and happiness, making sure we all communicate and share our lives and stories, encourage and cheer for each other. With our siblings chat group, which we keep active and informative amongst us siblings, separate from the other family group chats.

I have seen the hand of God in my sister Daisy's life. Her journey and faith is something I have said to her a few times that she needs to write a book. I will obviously summarize her journey but cannot do as much justice as if she would express it on her own. I will however do my best to summarize her journey and her faith.

"Restoration" is the nickname she and my dad came up with before she relocated to Australia in 2015. **1 Peter 5:10 ESV. And after you have suffered a little while, the God of all grace, who has called you to his eternal glory in Christ, will himself restore, confirm, strengthen, and establish you.**

1n 1992, months after graduating from high school. Daisy surprised the whole family stating she was pregnant. She had been dating this guy for about 6 months. This, I must be honest disappointed me, as if we were supposed to live a life under my parents roof together as close buddies forever. No one in the family was ready for this, we all felt she would be better served if she continued with her education, advance her academics, go to college or university. She felt like she had really disappointed my parents at the time. However, there was not many options to be had. Definitely abortion was not an option. Fortunately at the time, the guy who got her pregnant accepted and took responsibility. My parents insisted Daisy would not leave the home unless everything became formal and they got married. Being respected members of the community and church, I believe the idea of young Daisy falling pregnant and not being married was a big disappointment and not a good look in the neighborhood and community. Soon, there was a ceremony with few invited family members and friends and Daisy got married to Royson, the father of her first daughter Rutendo, he was 2 years her senior. They moved to Royson's family home in the same neighborhood not too far from where our house was, about a mile away. Suddenly, we did not have those daily conversations, listen to radio together, no more random card games, checkers or late nights watching TV and laughing on weekends. This obviously put a drift and strain in the relationship I had with her. Months later, my neice was born. Roy was extremely abusive, mentally and physically. This relationship and marriage did not last 2 years. Daisy returned home to my parents because it became toxic for her to stay in the relationship. My parents were happy to take her back home with their new grand child. Our crew was together again, Tendai, Daisy and myself. With the addition of our new little, Rutendo, who we were all excited to play with, feed and bond with.

Romans 12:12 ESV. Rejoice in hope, be patient in tribulation, be constant in prayer. In 1996, Daisy started dating Themba, he was a quiet and humble guy. Very respectful. He was complete opposite of Roy. Themba, Daisy and Rutendo started living together in Queensdale Harare after they got married. They had a child, my neice Anesu was born in 1997. They were a young happy family, working on growing their business, Themba was an electrician. One regular day in 1999, while driving from a job were he had gone earlier that day on a business trip to install electricity for a business. Themba was involved in a car accident, and lost his life instantly on the spot. This devastating and sudden death, left Daisy a widow and my two nieces without a father. Themba's death was so sudden, sad a painful. "Ro, why is this happening to me, why is God punishing me? I go to church, I pray, I tithe, I am loyal. I don't understand why this is happening to me." I felt her pain when she asked me these questions. I did not say much because I did not have an answer, all I could do was console her best I could at the time. **Mark 13:32–33 NIV—"But about the day or hour no one knows, not even the angels in heaven, nor the son, but only the father. Be on guard! Be alert! You do not know when that time will come.** Daisy was happy that she got a man who loved and respected her, and was not abusive in any way, a good provider, but losing him in such a sudden and calamitous manner, with no time to say good bye or parting words. She was devastated. This loss did something to her faith and it was difficult for anyone to make sense of it. She told me in tears one time as I was consoling her. "I trust God, only he has the answer. I will continue to pray and lean on him." We both shed tears as clutched and hugged. Daisy did not date or want to be in any relationship for the longest time after the death of Anesu's father. In the year 2000, I invited her to come to America. I wanted her to have a fresh start and be in a different environment, away from all the stress and to help her grieving process from losing Anesu's father in that fatal accident.

We applied for her to go to Nursing school in Washington DC and she was accepted, she moved to America, went to school, graduated her nursing program and started working. We had been attending a few churches but were not regular members of any particular church. My mother would ask us all the time which church we belonged to and that we should become members of a church. While living in Baltimore in 2006, a friend of hers invited her to Pastor Jamal Bryant's church. She went there one weekend and invited me to come the following weekend after she had enjoyed his powerful sermon and preaching. We became instant members and attendees. Pastor Jamal Bryant had a powerful preaching gift and remains a captivating and powerful pastor and is now lead pastor at New Birth Baptist Church in Atlanta. The only Sunday's Daisy or myself would miss was if we had to work. It became a norm. We invited a lot of our friends to his church as well. None were disappointed by his gift of preaching. Daisy attended Empowerment Temple Church almost every weekend to the very last Sunday before her eventual return to Zimbabwe. She worked so hard and raised money enough to build a house in Mainway Meadows, Harare. In 2008, she decided to move back to Zimbabwe because she had tried to apply for her children to come and live with her, unfortunately that did not work out, she missed her girls so much and just committed to go back to Zimbabwe. She filled up a 40 foot container with her furniture, business materials to start a beauty parlor, she packed lots of hair, nails, makeup, beauty supplies, she also shipped a vehicle to Zimbabwe for her return.

She had told me she was not happy and felt so hollow. She missed home, her children and my parents. "Chasing after money and working is not giving me happiness. I am going back home. I want to be there for my girls." She prayed and asked God for direction on what to do. Her decision to want to go back to Zimbabwe, though understandable was not easy, because she did not have a guaranteed income once she arrived back. Some friends and family tried to convince her not to leave and stay in America, but she said to me and everyone. "I will trust God to guide me and provide for me. He has brought me this far to support my girls and guided me with all I have. He will continue to provide for me when I return home." The final decision was hers and she started making arrangements and plans for her return to Zimbabwe. This whole time she was in America, her girls were living in Hatfield with my mom and dad, she would do all she could to send them all the latest fashion and gadgets, money and shoes, but still she felt the void and finally she realized she could not be apart from them any longer.

She arrived in Zimbabwe and moved in to the house she had built, she was happy to be back home with her girls. 2008 to 2015 Daisy did not have the best of experiences in the dating scene. No relationship would last or lead to anything. She would start to wonder if serious relationships or marriage was meant for her. She would tell me she feels like she is cursed. I pray to God all the time, I pray for a partner, a God fearing partner who is going to love me with my children. I do not want to grow old on my own. I would really feel the hurt and pain in her voice and how she would always cry out to God with that prayer. **Ecclessiastes 4:9–11 ESV—Two are better than one, because they have a good reward for their toil. For they fall, one will lift up his fellow. But woe to him who is alone when he falls and has not another to lift him up! Again, if two lie together, they keep warm, but how can one keep warm alone?**

In 2010, Daisy tells me she started having dreams of spiritual husband. She would wake up at times and start crying and praying to God for these dreams to stop. These nightmares and dreams carried on for the next three years.

She would pray and fast and ask her pastor to pray for her for these dreams to go away, and for a clear mind, one of her pastors I remember she spent a lot of time with and prayed for this problem to go away was Pastor Deke, he is a powerful man of God who I have listened to preach and attended his services a couple of times when I visited Zimbabwe. He was also one of the pastors at my sister Tendai's funeral. Daisy with the persistent help of this man of God prayed those dreams away. She had experienced these dreams for almost three years until the dreams just stopped after her persistence in prayer and believing to defeat those dreams and nightmares. **James 4:7 ESV—Submit yourself therefore to God. Resist the devil, and he will flee from you.** The dreams and nightmares have since stopped and she continues to pray against them and breaking any possible curses and evil deed they may have arisen from. Covering her children and family with prayer and protection against all evil and weapons formed against her or her offspring.

Ephisians 6:12 ESV—For we do not wrestle against flesh and blood, but against the rulers, against the authorities, against the cosmic powers over this present darkness, against the spiritual forces of evil in the heavenly places.

—Isaiah 54:17 ESV—No weapon that is fashioned against you shall succeed, and you shall confute every tongue that rises against you in judgement. This is the heritage of the servants of the Lord and their vindication from me, declares the Lord. 2011, the house burns down. Daisy was managing and running a butchery, supermarket and bottle store she was renting from my parents along with her other boutique business she was running in Harare. While she was at work one evening, Rutendo, Anesu and Kudzai and her maid were relaxing and in their bedrooms at her house. A loud bang was heard from the living room area, Rutendo went to check on it, To her shock, half the living room was engulfed in raging flames, She quickly rushed to alert the other occupants and they had no time to save any furniture, clothes or any personal belonging. As they all rushed out, the whole house was engulfed in flames. They stood out in helpless disbelief, not knowing what to do, in about 3 minutes they now describe, the whole roof was burning and then it caved in, everything burnt to the ground. Every piece of furniture and belonging was destroyed to ashes. The fire brigade came 30 minutes after the fire had started but there was nothing to salvage, it was only ashes and rubble. The one and only thing that survived in the whole house after they looked through the rubble, was the holy bible that Daisy kept on her night stand. Everything else in the house was turned to ashes. This was a most amazing thing to everyone who saw the damage and ravage, only the bible was intact.

When Daisy initially heard the news when she was at the store office, she fainted in disbelief. Apparently she had been fasting 3 days prior. She had finished her fast the day before. She again questioned why after being in deep prayer, God would respond to her prayers and fasting with a fire that destroyed everything she had worked for including her house and all the furniture that she had shipped from America, clothes and personal belongings she had worked for all her life. The only belongings her and her girls were the clothes they were wearing at the time. Daisy was in a pair of jeans and a Tshirt. She lost everything. I cannot even start to imagine what it is like to lose everything. This annihilation was another blow to Daisy, a calamitous event that set her back again. I do not know how she kept her sanity and strength, but after the crying, and sobbing, she tells me she prayed and asked God to lead her path and continued to believe in him. **1 Thessalonians 5:16–18 NIV Rejoice always, pray continually, give thanks in all circumstances, for this is God's will for you in Christ Jesus**. Mom and dad organized a prayer at their house with some of their church members the day after the fire, Daisy talks today of how the sermon the pastor preached to the attending family and friends solidified her faith and made her realize God was in control and does not make mistakes. He preached about the story of Job, wealthy as he was, had lost everything. His sons, his cattle and wealth, he remained in good standing with God and continued to trust in him, even his wife suggested he curse God, but Job continued to trust in the Lord. God restored Job again, double portion. Daisy says this story built her faith and was the reason she did not show much pain and hurt to everyone who was hearing her story, she remained calm and grateful that God had spared the lives of her daughters, and all the occupants of the house at the time. That all materials can be replaced but the lives of her children and all who were in the house were spared from injury or mishap. **John 10:10 KJV—The thief comes only to steal and kill and destroy, I have come that they may have life, and have it to the full.** Daisy remained faithful to God because though the the fire came to steal, kill and destroy, her rejoice was that the plan did not work and God spared the lives of everyone in the house. Victory was hers to celebrate. That one item that was salvaged from the cataclysmic fire, the Holy Bible became her new best friend again. She continued to pray and fast and attend church. One of our cousins sister, Aquinata went to visit Daisy at my parent's house a couple of days after the devastating fire that destroyed everything and she started crying out loud, feeling sorry and sad for Daisy. Daisy told her, "No sisi, don't cry, life is what is important, my daughters and everyone in the house survived, they came out on time.

God is good. We celebrate life. All that was lost can be replaced, God can and will restore me. I am grateful no life was lost and thank God for that. Do not cry. We lost every material thing yes, but God will restore us." **Job 1:21 NIV—"Naked I came from my mother's womb, and naked I will depart. The Lord gave and the Lord has taken away, may the name of the Lord be praised.** Is the verse she quoted to my cousin. When sister Aquinata told me this story, even when Daisy talked about her mindset back in that moment, I was touched and encouraged by the faith she had built and how she never looked at any of these incidents and retaliated against God, but it made her faith stronger. I could only admire that and have been proud of how she has kept the faith of a mustard seed, and kept praising God and believing in him in all tragedies and trials she had been through. Daisy received an overwhelming support from the parents, who let her and her children stay back at one of their three bedroom cottages rent free and utility free without paying them anything until she got back on her feet. All the siblings did much to support her materially, financially, and spiritually, including friends, family and church members. With the support, donations and gifts she received across the board from different people and friends made her feel whole again and was soon back on her feet. She has always kept the faith and she is the reason my faith has grown to the level it is because I have seen the hand of God and the blessings and rewards that have come her way because of always standing by the cross and believing, not wavering or questioning God or doubting his mercies and favor but being steadfast with her prayer and worship over the years. **James 1:12 ESV. Blessed is the man who remains steadfast under trial, for when he has stood the test he will receive the crown of life, which God has promised to those who love him.**

**Jeremiah 29:11 NIV—"For I know the plans I have for you,"
declares the Lord, "plans to prosper you and not to harm you, plans
to give you hope and a future.** After My nephew Tadiwa was in a freak
Australian football accident, he was studying Economics and Business
Development. He had an unfortunate accident that left him with a frac-
tured and broken leg. He was hospitalized, and around the same time daisy
was applying to study and improve her academic career, to leave Zimbabwe
again. She decided to expedite that application so she could also go and be
with Tadiwa in Australia and provide support for him. Anesu and Rutendo
are grown now and Daisy felt more comfortable leaving them behind compared to when she relocated to America fifteen years prior. She got accepted
to further her studies and relocated to Melbourne Australia in 2015.

Before her departure to Australia, before the ride to the airport after
prayers with mom, dad and a few family members, Daisy went and knelt
in front of my father and said, "Dad, I want you too bless me, I want to
go to Australia and start my new life, I want you to get married, and I
want you to bless me to find a good husband and get married." My dad is
not an ordained minister or pastor, this was the first time Daisy had made
such a gesture and request from my father, but dad played the role in this
powerful request from his daughter. I hear, he put his hands on her head
and said a prayer, preluding to her request and his well wishes for her safe
journey to Australia and next chapter in her life. Daisy travelled well and
adjusted well in Melbourne. She was welcomed and oriented to the city
by taka, my cousin and some of Tendai's close friends (Mudiwa, Dorcas,
Thelma, Tatenda, Kiri, all who when they met Daisy for the first time
cried and hugged in memory of their dear friend and sister to Daisy. They

continue to have a strong bond today. Daisy proceeded with her studies in health and worked on transferring her United States nursing credentials, and decided to further go to school and do social work classes to become a social worker.

Matthew 21:22 NIV—And whatever you ask in prayer, you will receive, if you have faith. In early 2017 Daisy met Munya. He is what she has been praying for. They clicked and started dating and have set been happily together ever since. Munya was introduced to the family and everyone liked him. A gentleman who Daisy is madly in love with. I personally spoke to Munya several times in 2017 and gave Daisy my seal of approval. We received a wedding invitation for Daisy and Munya end of 2018. Their wedding was May 4, 2019 in Melbourne. I was fortunate to be able to travel to Australia and stayed for one month, seeing the beautiful country, city hopping, site seeing, connecting with cousins Taka and Brighton. Above all representing my parents for the wedding. They had great support from their church members and friends. I was happy to see the life Daisy continues to live with her husband, being involved members in their church and how they attend church events, and prayer meetings during the week. A praying, God fearing couple that I wish well and that they have an eternity together. The couple is happily married and enjoying life together. I am so happy to see the journey Daisy has travelled and, regardless of the setbacks, she has remained steadfast on the cross and kept the faith. (You inspire me Daisy). You have the faith of a mustard seed my dear sister.

Daisy's stubborn faith and prayers have helped me in my personal, faith, growth in Christ. I have seen God work miracles in her life. With her constant prayer and belief. In his time. **Ecclesiastes 3:11 NIV—He has made everything beautiful in his time. He has also set eternity in the human heart, yet no one can fathom what God has done from beginning to end.**

—Isaiah 54:17 ESV—No weapon that is fashioned against you shall succeed, and you shall confute every tongue that rises against you in judgement. This is the heritage of the servants of the Lord and their vindication from me, declares the Lord.

CHAPTER NINE

Final Word and Conclusion

As much as I have given a snapshot of my life and summary of my journey and path to where I am today. My faith and belief in God, growing up in a Christian background and growing up in the church. I have had moments and large phases of my life where I have definitely lost my ways, and strayed away from the Lord. May have been due to my surroundings, peer pressure, being in high school and wanting to withhold a status and image of being stoic and show the world that I was on top and nothing would rattle me, presenting an image of macho mentality. Being a people person but at the same time wanting to be maintain that "cool guy" status, so going to church and praying was not the cool thing to always do. I could give several examples where I chose to please the world and be of the world rather than go to church or bible study or remain on the Godly path. In high school when I started going out to clubs, parties and started consuming alcohol with the boys just to be cool guy and maintain an image. I am fortunate to have turned down drugs and narcotics that could have led me down an unrecoverable path. I would say no to the drugs, I guess in fear of what would happen if I ended up not being able to stop, or for them ruining my life, or simply not to disappoint my parents or family. I would remember hearing my father tell me all my life. "Don't do drugs." His voice would ring in my head whenever anyone offered me anything. The fear of disappointing my parents and the idea that I may get hooked up and ruin my life kept me in check, therefore the most I ever did and could do was alcohol or a beer every now and again at parties or functions. This idea of not wanting to do drugs made me choose friends who had the same mentality and were not going to influence me to start.

I carried this mentality throughout college and to this day, I avoid any association or company of people that I know do entertain drugs or may influence me to go down that path. I still hear my dad's voice telling me drugs will not benefit me in anything and I should never do them. I however will still have the occasional beer and drink. I have never been a heavy drinker, and can go three months or longer without touching a drink of alcohol, and I surely do not miss it when I do not have it.

Not everyone reacts the same exact way when it comes to the covid-19. The symptoms do vary and are not the exact same for every individual. Some people are asymptomatic, some end up on a ventilator, some are unfortunate not to make it and it takes their life. Because this virus is new to everyone, and has only been around since end of 2019. No certain cure or vaccine has been developed. There has been several remedies and possible suggestions and preventative measures to either prevent the spread of the disease and contaminating it, or helping to reduce the symptoms.

Social distancing—Avoid being in close proximity with other individuals. Keeping a safe distance of about 6 feet from the next person if you do have to be out and around other people.

Wearing a mask—It is airborne spread, and wearing masks prevents or reduces the spread of air particles and droplets that could be spread to the next person if one is infected or vice versa, to prevent catching it if you do not have it and an infected person in your proximity breathes or talks, emitting the airborne particles your way. The mask helps prevent you from being infected. Or infecting others if you are infected.

Hand washing—Good personal hygiene and hand washing is recommended, avoiding touching the face and mucosa, such as eye, nose, mouth. These are possible openings where the virus can enter your body.

Cleaning of surfaces—avoid touching surfaces that may have a lot of human activity or human contact, Such as shopping carts, door handles, counters. If you have to handle these surfaces, attempt to clean or sanitize them, have readily available hand wipes or alcohol based gel/sanitizers to try and disinfect your hands temporarily until you get an opportunity to wash your hands thoroughly.

Avoid crowded places—Wherever you have a large gathering or crowded place, there are possible chances and high probability that someone in the crowd may be infected, and because it is not easy to maintain the recommended distancing in such areas, it is better to avoid them. Possible crowded areas places such, bars, lounges, night clubs, stadiums, churches, classrooms.

Blood types... Some research and studies has shown that people with "O" Blood type have a higher resistance to the virus and show less symptoms if they contract it. This is just informative because one cannot change their blood type. If you are born with blood type A or B, for example you cannot go to a blood bank and request a change of blood type and transform to type O, so the best advice is to follow the guidelines and recommendations from health professionals and experts in the area and region you live in to avoid the spread of the virus and prevent yourself from catching it.

Hopefully someone will come up with a vaccine soon, estimation of that happening is early part of the year 2021. My prayer and hope is by then, the spread of this virus will be curtailed, and maybe herd immunity will be achieved by then. Herd immunity is when a large number of the population builds immunity (through vaccination or previous infection and build of antibodies) to an infectious disease that reduces further risk and reduction in transmission to the community or eliminating it altogether.

As a general practice, exercise and maintaining good health is recommended for wellness. Prevention is definitely better than cure. If one can avoid getting the virus altogether, looking after oneself and being smart and careful about their surroundings, practicing social distancing and other methods described above. This will go a long way in helping prevent the disease from spreading and flattening the curve in areas where the virus and infections are spreading and spiking.

Exercising daily if you can, this helps keep your lungs active and healthy. There are 1440 minutes in a day, dedicate at least 30 of those to exercise or working out. Health is wealth. Doing breathing exercises to strengthen your lungs or meditation. Simply staying in shape, taking your vitamins and eating healthy.

Stay challenged and doing things and activities that keep you informed and keep your mind active, read books, make friends, find mentors or a mentor (someone who challenges you or you look up to), balance your life and always do what is right. Love all people and races, do not hate, learn to forgive, be at peace, laugh, smile, find a hobby, be it golf, hiking, cycling, reading or whatever you choose, be diverse, be happy, above all, ask God to give you guidance and to protect you from the evils of this world and anyone who has ill will against you. **Psalm 32:15 NIV—My times are in your hands, deliver me from the hands of my enemies, from those who pursue me.** Return to sender. Go for it, ask for what you want and work towards achieving it. Have faith, believe in your thoughts and inner drive.

Pray for what you are wanting, declare it, and receive it, work towards achieving your goals, expect nothing to be handed to you on a platter, but work hard towards achieving what you want. **Matthew 7:7–8 NIV Ask and it will be given to you, seek and you will find, knock and the door will be opened to you. For everyone who asks receives, the one who seeks finds, and the one who knocks, the door will be opened.** Envision the outcome and visualize victory. Plan for the future, work towards your goals. We can only envision the future and believe. **Hebrews 11:1 NIV-Now faith is confidence in what we hope for and assurance about what we do not see.** Faith is what does it, it helps give peace of mind and clears the path. The PAST is history, we cannot change it, the FUTURE is a mystery, only God knows how it will play out. Be grateful for today and give thanks, the gift of the PRESENT moment. We can only be thankful for the present, pray and believe for the future. The power of FAITH, and what an amazing powerful GOD we serve. Full of love and mercy. The light at the end of the tunnel, push forward and receive it. Remember, faith with no works is dead. 'THE MIND IS A POWERFUL THING. **Proverbs 23:7 KJV—For as he thinketh in his soul, so is he. / Change your mind and you will change your life.**

One situation that led me to question God and his existence. The one time I distinctly remember when my faith was rock bottom and felt hopeless, and could not understand why God let me down. Was the day I lost my little sister and weeks that followed after her passing. Why? Why Tendai? I never understood why she was taken so early from this earth. She was so loving, caring, warm, bubbly and everyone found her to be the most amazing, warm, and happy person. "Why does God take away good people?" I asked. The day she was admitted, I prayed, we prayed. Everything happened so fast and when the doctors informed me of her passing, besides being numb and confused. I felt deserted and abandoned by God. Only to come full circle after so many emotions including anger, that God was and still remains in control. I only got consoled by the holy spirit. Scripture and prayers from pastors, friends and family prayed with me and gave me strength to refocus. The word of God, verses and scripture I would hear made me come around and changed the anger I had for God to trusting him and believing he does not make mistakes. As I got ready to travel with her body back to Zimbabwe from Atlanta, I was strong and full of faith and believed God would give me strength, sanity and guidance to travel across the ocean with the body of my little sister, to take her back home to sleep in the Lord.

Isaiah 57:1–2 NLT Good people pass away, the godly often die before their time. But no one seems to care or wonder why. No one

seems to understand that God is protecting them from the evil to come. For those who follow godly paths will rest in peace when they die. I find comfort to this day, that my little sister is sleeping in the arms of the Lord. She will never experience any pain or disappointment or mishaps or any negativity on this earth again. I am at peace and will continue to trust in God. May your soul continue to sleep in peace Tendai. Rest in power.

To sum it all up, I cannot tell anyone what to believe in or say negative about anyone who believes in any other faith, religion or practice. I can only speak of my experiences or the path I have travelled and my Christian faith and belief, what has worked for me and I find to be my guiding light. My path. I have been fortunate to learn and read about different religions, beliefs and faiths, but as for me and my family, we will trust and serve God. I have come full circle in my life and realize now more than ever. There is no greater power. I have so much to be thankful and grateful for. I have been brought from the brink of death, from a three day coma, from sickness that the medical experts had done everything they could, but lost hope in treatment and threw in the towel, giving up on my healing potential. I have been healed and cured from the covid-19 with days of artificial oxygen being administered to me under critical and intensive care. I thank God for giving me the opportunity to write this book and sharing my experiences and showing God's everlasting love.

He is a powerful, healing and faithful God who is full of grace and mercy. I will forever praise and worship him.

Amen.

ACKNOWLEDGEMENTS

To my mother Mildred (Only I call you Midhu), I want to thank you for being the praying warrior of our family, you made sure we attended church and Sunday school when I was young, you taught me how to love, you are warm, caring and love all your children, grandchildren and family with no reservation. You are an amazing woman and I thank God for you every day. To dad (Mdilo) you are the pillar of our family, thank you for teaching me to be the man I am today, your love, compassion, hard work, dedication and sacrifices you took for all your children and extended family. You taught me how to be a proud, humble and respectful man. I want to say thank you. To my siblings. Choice, Paul, Godwin, Daisy, Tendai, you all have played a significant part in my life and I thank you for all the life lessons, laughter, joy, and lessons of this life. You taught me how to compete, to be tough, to fight for what I wanted. Though as the second youngest child, I got away with a lot more and got more favors and protection. I thank you. To my children, Panashe, Kurai and Kayla. I love you so much, I am so proud of you and I pray you continue to make me proud. May you always be protected and covered by the blood of Jesus. Long life and happiness to you all. To my dear wife, Madelien. I feel like the luckiest man on this earth to have you as my wife, thank you for being my friend, a great mother to our children, a partner in everything. For just being you. I love you forever and look forward to growing old and grey with you, taking our grandchildren to activities and soccer games or whatever path they chose, (Chie baby). To all my nieces, nephews, cousins, uncles, aunts, in-laws and everyone who has played a part in my life, upbringing, teachers, coaches, pastors, friends, I want to say thank you.

ABOUT THE AUTHOR

MARRIED, FATHER OF three, Rodgers was born in Zimbabwe and raised in a Christian faith home. He relocated to the USA for college after high school and lived a life with no parameters or boundaries in the college years— diverse paths, with heavy alcohol consumption and party life, putting the faith and Christian path on hold while enjoying life to the fullest. He turned away from the faith and godly path he was raised in to almost a life of no prayer and belief until the major motorcycle accident in 2004 left him in a coma for three days. That was a turning point and change of direction in how he lived. He got married, became a good husband and father to his children, and turned the full cycle to raising his children in the same Christian faith he himself was raised in, to become credible and respected individuals in the society with principles of hard work, faith, respect, leadership, and love. He lived and enjoyed life full of abundance and joy. Fast forward to contracting the COVID-19 (coronavirus) in April of 2020, he survived a week of critical care and hospitalization. The theme in all near-death experiences throughout his life was to show the power of faith, that God remains in control, and what we put our mind to and believe in, with the strong and right mindset, what we think and believe will have powerful outcomes. The mind is a powerful thing.

LinkedIn: Rodgers Masuta
Twitter: @RodSutas
IG: Rod Sutas
FB: Rod Sutas

www.ingramcontent.com/pod-product-compliance
Lightning Source LLC
Chambersburg PA
CBHW021650120626
46545CB00002B/786